EVERYBODY KNOWS THAT,

Don't They?

Alan Easley

NukeWorks
Publishing

NukeWorks Publishing
Fulton, Mo 65251 USA

ISBN 978-0-9825294-3-0

Cover design by Justin Easley
Cover illustration and photos by Hannah Portwood.
hdaley764@gmail.com
She did a nice job.

Illustration for "Damn Virus!" by Hannah Portwood
Other Illustrations by Kristin Kijowski kijowski27@yahoo.com
Photo Scanning by Kim Small editorkim@gmail.com

Some stories have been previously published in various magazines, etc.
These stories are used with permission of the original publishers.

All photos used with permission of their respective owners.

Printed in U.S.A.

IN MEMORY

I've known James Earl Grant since High School, and we lived neighbors it seems like forever. Our farms joined, we rented ground together over the years, he round baled hay for me, I helped him mow and rake, and occasionally I'd help him catch up on square baling. We've sorted and hauled cattle together, and chased strays from I-70 to Deer Park. There were 2 or 3 that either died somewhere of old age or someone else sold them, but when we went after them we usually found them and brought them home. The neighborhood is sure 'nuff going to have a big hole in it from now on.

ACKNOWLEDGEMENTS

This is the third book my Grandson Justin has helped me with. Once again he laid out the pages, designed the cover, and pushed all of the magic buttons necessary to get a book ready for publication. I really don't know what I'd do without him.

I was visiting with my some-sort-of-a-cousin Steve Cheavens and his wife Carolyn one evening, when I mentioned that what with everyone working and raising families, it was kind of hard to find someone to do my typing. Carolyn said she could probably help me out some with that, and she damn sure did! (She talked Steve into typing all of it.) THANKS, CAROLYN.

By the time I started writing picture captions I didn't want to ask Steve to do any more, so I sort of coerced my sister, Virginia DeMarce, into volunteering to type captions. Thanks, Sis.

A close family friend, Kristin Kijowski, volunteered to do some illustrations for the book, and they came out really nice. I think the drawings add a lot to the stories they are used with. THANKS, KRISTIN.

Kim Small of Free Range Publishing scanned all of the photos.

Hannah Portwood took the photo for the back cover and did the illustration for the front cover.

Some stories were previously published in Farm Collector and Heritage Iron, and I appreciate Editors Leslie McManus and Sherry Schaefer giving me permission to reprint them.

Also, thanks to Cindy Stewart, Russel Sapp, Zane Dodge, and Richard Sorrels for digging through their old pictures and finding the ones I needed. I think that the pictures add a lot to any story.

When it gets right down to the nitty-gritty, I really didn't do a whole lot myself, just kind of remembered a few things and jotted them down. Everyone else did all of the hard work and I just sat back and watched them do it!

INTRODUCTION

When I started working on this book, someone asked me if I was changing any names to protect the innocent. I replied that I didn't need to, because no one mentioned in this book is innocent of anything.

I'm sure I've mentioned some people you haven't thought of for many years, and maybe some that you've never even heard of, but hopefully when you read about them, it will bring a smile to your face. And maybe some of these stories will make you remember something that you did "once upon a time" that was just as dumb as some of the things I've written about. Anyhow, if things like this never happened, life would be pretty damn dull, which thankfully it's not.

When I wrote my 1st book, I had the title long before the book was finished. I had the title for my 2nd book before I ever started writing. However, this book was at least 90% done and it still wasn't titled. Not long before James Earl Grant passed away we were visiting one afternoon when I asked him, "Did you hear about ---?" (Whatever it was) and he replied, "Well yeah, I figured everybody had heard about that by now." I grabbed an auction flyer off the table, flipped it over, and quickly wrote down several variations of his answer. By the time I got home I had my title; Everybody Knows That: Don't They?

Derrick Goold, sportswriter for the St. Louis Post-Dispatch, provided this quote from an unidentified professor at the M.U. School of Journalism: "If you cannot write well, you better learn to write a lot." And when you can't do either one this is what you get. I hope you enjoy it.

FOREWORD

Like Alan Easley, I grew up surrounded by my parents and grandparents on a farm where stories of my ancestors and neighbors were regularly shared with my brother, Bob, and me throughout our growing up years. This telling of our family's and town's history was a regular part of time spent with my grandparents whether we were visiting in the yard, at family dinners, or during Sunday Drives.

When I was introduced to Alan's first book in 2014 at a Missouri River Regional Library author event, I knew my father, Richard, would relate to Alan's stories and I gave the book to him for his birthday. Little did I know, how closely Dad would personally relate to Alan. So much so, Dad called Alan to tell him how much he enjoyed his writing and a quick friendship was formed. Dad told me that Alan's life was not so unlike his own in Illinois. Dad said there were few people who understood what it was like to farm in a different time the way he and Alan had. As a librarian, I love connecting books and readers so when I paired Dad with Alan's book, you could say it was a true success.

In Alan's third set of stories, he describes more of his farm life experiences from rural America with all the same warmth and humor of his first two books. These stories make one long for simpler days, when you knew your neighbors and they knew you and your parents and grandparents and where they lived and what they did. Pull up a chair and get comfortable; Alan's storytelling is one of a kind.

Claudia (Young) Cook
Illinois native, daughter of a farmer, and director of the Missouri River Regional Library

EVERYBODY KNOWS THAT,

Don't They?

Life on the Farm

When Jeff was a kid farm work wasn't something he looked forward to, he just did it because I said, "Get your butt on that tractor and disk, dammit!" One afternoon I was planting beans on Leroy Sapp's farm, and Jeff was disking in the big bottom at Schwabe's. The next morning I started planting in the big bottom, and at the north end where the creek runs along the edge of the field, I noticed disk marks running right up to the creek. I stopped and looked the situation over, and it appeared that Jeff had gotten too close to the bank and hung the edge of the disk over the creek for about 10 feet before he had pulled away. When I asked him about it he replied, "I just dozed off for a minute, it didn't hurt anything." No, but it damn sure could have!

* * * * *

At least Jeff wasn't as bad as John Massey. John told me that the morning after he graduated from High School he was plowing in the river bottom on his Dad's farm near Lebanon Missouri, when he fell asleep and drove an "M" Farmall and a three-bottom plow into the river, where it turned upside down before settling to the bottom. John said that wasn't one of his prouder moments.

* * * * *

Years ago, I was driving down Rangeline Road one afternoon when Turner Vemer pulled out of Bowling Lane. He flagged me down and asked if I had time to go to his house, pick up his Allis Chalmers 170 and hay bine, and take it to the Roth place for him. He said he would pick me up in a few minutes and take me back to my truck.

I told him I could probably handle that and he said to be careful, because if I hit a pothole the front wheels might "shimmy a little." I picked up the tractor and headed north on Rangeline Road and before long I hit a pothole. "Shimmy a little," hell! The front wheels started flopping back and forth so bad I thought the whole front end would fall off before I got slowed down. I had to stop completely before the wheels quit flopping. It happened twice more before I got to the Roth place.

When Turner picked me up I remarked that if he'd go to Henderson Implement Company Henry Semon probably had some tie rod ends in stock that would fit the 170. He replied that they didn't really need replacing, because it wasn't a problem once he got to the field. Turner was just trying to live up to his nickname. James Earl Grant always referred to him as old T. A. T. for "tight assed Turner."

*   *   *   *   *

One year Mrs. Schwabe had contracted Larry Cook to lime her place at the east end of Turner Farm Road. One afternoon late Larry started to pull into the little field back of the rental house. As he went through the gate the long-haired hippie who lived there came running out in his underwear, waving his arms and hollering. He told Larry that he couldn't come into that field. Larry told the hippie that Mrs. Schwabe wanted that field limed, and he was damn sure going to lime it. He said he ran over a lot of tall, funny looking weeds while he was spreading that little patch. Larry sure ruined that poor old hippies cash crop!

*   *   *   *   *

Recently I plowed a food plot for Greg with my old MM 670 Super and a 4-bottom mounted Ford plow. It really made me appreciate the hydraulic system on all of the Ford tractors that I owned over the years. I've got a feeling that most of the plowing done with Molines was done with semi-mounted or pull type plows, because using that mounted S.O.B. sure isn't real satisfactory. If my arms were 18 inches longer so I could reach the hydraulic controls without bending over it would help a bunch.

*   *   *   *   *

One year when I was pretty small wheat harvest in Boone County was a total mess. The ground was pretty soft that summer, and pea vines had come through the wheat. At that time Pappy had an 8N Ford tractor and a PTO driven Case combine. The 8N just didn't have enough power to pull through the mud and run the combine with all those green vines going through, and Pappy spent half his time digging out plugs.

He finally got his cousin Wat Cheavens and Wat's son Tom to finish cutting the wheat. They had a John Deere combine with an engine on it that they pulled with a two-cylinder John Deere tractor, probably a G, but it could've been an A. Either way, I thought that was a big son of a bitch. I never turned into a John Deere fan, but back then that popping did sound kinda neat.

Later that same year Pappy got Wat and Tom to pick some corn for him. It was on the Nifong farm east of Highway 63, where Lenoir Retirement Center and Lenoir Nursing Home are located now. They had a John Deere 2-row picker mounted on the same tractor they had cut wheat with. It kept Pappy and Leon Winfrey busy, pulling wagon loads of corn from the field to the farm on Bearfield Road, and hand scooping it into the cribs.

$$*\quad*\quad*\quad*\quad*$$

John Paul Allen's Dad, J. David Allen, was raised on a farm on what is now Bass Lane east of the KOMU TV Tower, where he lived his entire life. The original settlers called the area "Frog Prairie." There were no trees, just Native Prairie Grass as far as you could see. John Paul said his dad told him that the old timer's commented that if the ground was ever plowed they would be fighting sprouts forever more, and they were right. The area now has as many Cedar trees, thorn sprouts, and other trees as anywhere else in the County.

Mr. Allen was raised by his Uncle and Aunt, Clarence and Mattie Fischer. Back when I rented his farm I was visiting with him one afternoon when he told me about the time when he was 12/14 years old and the grown-ups went somewhere for the weekend, leaving him home to plow with a team and walking plow.

Running across the farm generally east to west was a low, natural drainage area covered with a thick stand of Native Prairie Grass. Mr. Allen said it was a lot easier just to plow through that low area, rather than laying the plow on its side, skidding it across and then setting it back up and getting it in line, so plow through it is what he did. When Mr. Allen's Uncle got home and saw what had been done, he said "Boy, you've ruined it! Grass won't never grow there again, there'll be a ditch so deep you can't see out of it." He was close to right. It's not that deep, but it's waist deep or more in most places, and 8' to 10' wide.

Mr. Allen told me that he thought a lot of times over the years how much better it would have been if he had laid that plow on its side and skidded it across that low swog, instead of taking the easy way out. He was an interesting old gentleman. I wish I had spent more time listening to his stories when I had the chance.

* * * * *

The best I can remember J. David Allen was the last person in our area to plant with a team. He had an H Farmall that he used for tillage, but he planted with a team and a 2-row planter. He rented part of the Watson place on Gans Road one year when I was 10 or 12 years old, and I thought it was really interesting to watch him turn that team around and get the planter lined up for the next pass.

* * * * *

Back in the early 80s, when James Earl Grant first started selling Cargill seed as a sideline, Company Rep David Brummet asked James Earl to plant a seed corn test plot at the corner of Rangeline and Turner Farm Road. Cargill had good seed, and this was a high-profile location, where the test plot could easily be seen from two roads.

I don't remember why, but at the time we decided it would be best if I planted the plots with my 6-row Ford planter. It was a plate type planter, so every variety of seed was supposed to be the same size, so all we would have to do was vacuum the left-over seed out of the boxes, refill, and plant. After I planted 12 rows of the first variety, Brummet said "Alan, the next variety is a different size, you'll have to change plates." I wasn't really happy about it, but I removed the boxes from the planter, turned them upside down, removed the four bolts holding the bottom on each box, changed plates and reassembled everything. I made a round, and when I stopped at the end Brummet said "You'll have to change plates again, this size is different too." I said "Brummet, what the F – – – is going on?' He replied, "they must've thought you had a plateless planter, because every variety is a different size."

I jerked the boxes off the planter, changed plates and slammed them back on. By the time I did this five more times I was about 200% pissed off! I was cussing Brummett for organizing the test plot, Cargill for screwing up the seed size, James Earl for wanting me to plant the damn plots, myself for owning a plate -type planter, and the world in general. Eight varieties X six rows = 48 plate changes, with 4 bolts per box each time = 192 damn bolts I changed. I might've already mentioned that I was pissed off!

It must've made an impression on Brummet. When David Grant's daughter Maddie graduated from M.U. in 2017, there was a reception for her in Grant's machine shed. I was setting with Bob Grant and James Edward Ballenger when Brummet walked up to our table. I hadn't seen him for 30 years, but he stuck out his hand and said "Alan, David Brummet. Have you planted any test plots lately?"

*   *   *   *   *

When New Holland first started building big round balers it took people a while to figure out how to move all those bales. The first year James Earl Grant had a big round baler he baled a couple of hundred bales of weedy Timothy for me on Monroe Lanham's farm, at the corner of Route Z and I 70. When fall came the bales were still sitting in the field.

I was wintering a bunch of cows at home that year, so I bought a good three P.H. bale spike and started moving the bales home one at a time with my 5000 Ford tractor. I was feeding two bales a day and it took over 30 minutes per trip, so I would haul two bales and feed them, then make two more trips and stockpile them. That left the rest of the day to feed at Pappy's and do other chores.

Before winter was over I bought a heat-houser and put it on the 5000, which made running back and forth in zero weather a little more bearable. By spring I'd worn most of the good off a set of rear tires. Now people haul six bales at a time on self-dumping trailers, or haul 15 or 20 per load on a gooseneck. Equipment sure has improved over the years.

*   *   *   *   *

In 1980 Marcia and I went to the State Fair in Sedalia one Saturday with Bill and Doris Blackwell. Bill and I were wandering through the machinery exhibits when I spotted a trailer on display that was designed to haul four big round bales. It was built by a company in California, Missouri. I talked to the vendor about the trailer, and after telling me what a great little trailer it was he said there was a State Fair special on all week, and the trailer was only $850. I told him I was riding with a neighbor and I wouldn't ask him to pull the trailer home behind his station wagon. After he found out I was from Columbia he told me that MFA had one of the trailers in stock. Monday morning I went to MFA in Columbia and bought the trailer for $800. State Fair special my ass!

*   *   *   *   *

Me unloading bales off the little trailer at the old farm on Bearfield Road.

That was the first big-bale trailer in our neighborhood; there's no telling how many bales of hay were hauled on that thing. It seems like I hauled a million, plus Ronnie Smith borrowed it numerous times and hauled hay everywhere from The Devil's Backbone to Harrisburg. My youngest son Jeff and Randy Blackwell worked for Ron Roberts one year, and they used it to haul a bunch of hay for Ron. Carl Fritchey borrowed it several times, and finally used it for a pattern and built one about like it. The trailer had about 1000 pounds of welding rod gobbed on it in various places, but it was still in one piece when I sold the last of my cattle in 2015. I had some big bales left that I sold to Clifford Montgomery for his buffalo and he used the trailer to haul the hay he bought. When he left with the last load he had also bought the trailer to go with it.

Me and the little trailer. State Fair special, my ass!

*   *   *   *   *

Note: This story was first published in the May/June 2018 issue of Heritage Iron and is reprinted with permission

When I was crop farming, my two main tractors were an 8600 Ford and a 9600 Ford, so I really enjoyed the article about the restored 9600 in the January/February issue of *Heritage Iron*. The ad in the classified section of the same issue for an 8600 Ford with a seized engine also got my attention.

I used to salvage, and occasionally restore, old abandoned tractors in my spare time. My two sons, two or three of my grandsons, and a couple of neighbors were usually ready to help on any project that came along. However, I'm now 75 years old, my grandsons are grown and in the service or working and raising a family, and the last salvage project I was involved in – four or five years ago – actually seemed more like work than it did fun.

When Zane Dodge, a neighbor who has helped me on numerous projects over the years, called and asked if I'd seen the ad about the 8600, it really piqued my interest. My first phone call pinpointed the location of the tractor as about a five-hour drive from home. After thinking about it overnight, I decided to try it "one more time", so I called again and made an offer on the tractor, which was accepted. Since it was close to Christmas, we agreed that I would pick the tractor up after the first of the year. I put a check in the mail and after several raised eyebrows and one "Old man, what in the world were you thinking about?", I settled in to enjoy the holidays.

In the days leading up to Christmas, my son, Greg, and I unloaded some white oak 6"x6" and some 1"x 6" fencing planks that had been on my trailer for quite a while. The lights on the back of my truck had been coming and going for several months, so the prospect of a road trip gave me the incentive to do some rewiring on the truck. I made sure I had plenty of chains and boomers in the toolbox, and by the first of the year, everything was ready to go. However, the weather and several other minor distractions got in the way, so it was the 13th of March before I finally headed to Nebraska to get the tractor. Longtime friend "Big John" McCray went with me. John and I worked construction together years ago, and we rehashed old memories for the entire 598-mile round trip.

The previous owner pushed the 8600 onto my trailer using a big Allis-Chalmers with a front-end loader, then we cinched the 8600 down for the ride home. At one time, I would have left home early, loaded the tractor and returned home in the same day, but it's not "at one time" anymore, so John and I left at 11:00 a.m. and after the tractor was loaded, we got a motel room, ate way more than we needed, and then got a good night's rest before returning home the next day.

I picked this 8600 Ford up in Dunbar, NE. Hopefully I'll have enough sense to make it the last one, but probably not. March 2018.

The trip was uneventful, which is always the best kind, and there's now a non-running 8600 Ford setting at my house. I have absolutely no idea why I have it, but it's been fun so far and I'm sure I'll think of a use for it eventually.

Note: Bobby Baumgartner Jr. saw the tractor sitting in my barn lot, and he wanted it more than I did, so he is now the proud owner.

*   *   *   *   *

Note: Originally published in FARM COLLECTOR. Used with permission.

When I was growing up in the late 1940s and early 50s we hauled rocks on what Grandpap called a mud boat – about the same thing as a stone boat but with a different name.

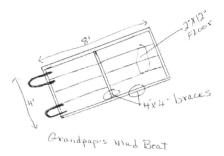

Grandpap's Mud Boat

Grandpap and Pappy built it out of rough sawed 2 x 12 white oak planks. It had oak 4 x 4's bolted on top of the planks, front, back and one across the center for added strength, and one down each side. The front of the 2 x 12's were sawed on a 45° angle to keep it from digging in quite so bad. I remember we always loaded it heavy on the rear for the same reason. It wasn't curved up in front like the factory built one pictured in the August 2017, issue of Farm Collector. A couple of heavy flat straps, salvaged from some old piece of equipment, had been bent into a U shape at the blacksmith shop and bolted to the front of the sled as hooks for pull chains.

Every field on the farm had at least one rocky spot, and when Pappy was plowing with the old 9N Ford and a

2-bottom plow, Grandpap and I would pick and pile rocks. When the rocks were eventually all piled, Grandpap would hitch his team to the mud boat and we would haul rocks. The team of Blacks, Buckshot and Dodi, were the last horses on the farm, and they stayed around until they died of old age. I don't know why Grandpap chose to keep this pair. He said they ran off when they were young, and spent the rest of their lives waiting for a good chance to do it again. They were so crazy that my sister and I weren't allowed in the barn lot if the horses were there, but after getting them hitched to the mud boat Grandpap would say "We're all right now, Cap. They can't run in loose dirt when they're pulling a load of rocks."

*   *   *   *   *

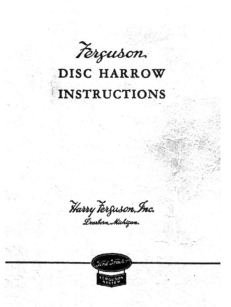

Hauling rocks wasn't the only thing we used the mud boat for. Pappy had a six-foot Ferguson disk he had bought to use with his 9N Ford tractor. The disk didn't have wheels, it attached to the 3-point hitch on the tractor, but when you raised the lift arms it didn't lift the disk, it merely removed the angle from the gangs to make turning in loose ground a little easier. However, there was still the problem of moving the disk on the road. Pappy would drive across the mud boat from the rear and stop when the disk was pretty well centered. The mud boat wasn't hitched directly to the tractor, it pulled through the disk. Pappy would loop a short chain around the disk tongue and hook up to the pull loops on the mud boat. A couple of miles on those old creek gravel roads ground a lot of wood off the bottom of the mud boat, but lumber was cheaper than disk blades, and a lot easier to replace.

Hitch linkage on a Ferguson disc.

*   *   *   *   *

One wet fall I was cutting beans at Leroy Sapp's farm in the little field east of Leroy's house, by the Gillespie Family Cemetery. It was pretty muddy and I was kind of pushing my luck, and I eventually stuck my 303 International. When I tried to back up the splines stripped out in the coupler between the transmission and final drive, and I had no power to the drive wheels. I knew that the combine would pull pretty hard since it was deadweight, so I got R. J. Estes to bring his 4020 John Deere, and J. R. Jacobs brought his 170 Allis Chalmers. We got hooked up, and the two tractors had no problem pulling me to solid ground. We were standing around talking after we unhooked the chains, when J. R. suddenly asked "Sapp, are those turnips over there?" Leroy allowed as how they were, so J. R. walked over to the patch and started peeling and eating raw turnips and slipping a few of the better ones in his pockets. Leroy watched him for a minute, then said "Alan, by the time Jacobs gets done stripping my turnip patch I could've hired you a wrecker cheaper!" J. R. just kept on pulling turnips.

*   *   *   *   *

When I was farming the Schwabe place I always had to be really careful in the creek bottoms, because there were places where you'd wind up belly deep in the mud so fast it wasn't funny, wondering what the hell just happened.

There was a seep in the 14-acre field that Mrs. Schwabe referred to as "the hog bottom" that was pretty much always wet. It wasn't real big, maybe 50 feet wide by 150 feet long, but it would sure bury your ass. One year Greg was cultivating beans in the hog bottom during July. It hadn't rained for over a month and when Greg came to the seep he thought it would be a lot easier to drive across it than to turn around every time. He raised the cultivator and got about halfway across before the wheels spun one time, the tractor sank, and all of the cultivator shovels dug into the ground. By the time he got the tractor shut off water was oozing out of the ruts.

There were no cell phones back then so Greg walked about a mile to get to a phone, but when he called the house Marcia wasn't home. Luckily he caught Tekotte at home and Jay rounded up a couple of long chains and came to Schwabe's on his 3020 John Deere. Greg and Jay had to unhitch from the cultivator before they could get the tractor out, and then they hooked the chain on the cultivator and drug it out. Of course, it turned upside down while they were dragging it and by the time they righted the cultivator and got it hitched back on my 7600 Ford it had turned into quite a project. When they finally got done Jay said "Boy, there's a wet spot there, I believe you ought to go around it from now on." It kinda hurt Greg's pride to get his Ford pulled out by a John Deere, but under the circumstances he didn't complain too much.

*   *   *   *   *

That fall Bill Schuler and I were cutting beans in the hog bottom. Bill had a 45 John Deere combine, and I had a 303 International. We would cut up to the edge of the seep, then stop and back out and turn around. I was headed west, and Bill was headed east with that 150-foot-long seep in between us. We stopped at the same time, shifted into reverse and when we let out the clutches both combines spun their wheels and sank at the same time. Again, water oozed up around the wheels. Schuler climbed down off his combine and looked the situation over, then said "Easley, you dumb bastard, don't you have enough sense not to drive so damn close to a seep?"

My New Holland combine. The duals helped most of the time, but not in the seeps. July 1981.

*   *   *   *   *

There's some weird dirt on that old farm. Less than ¼ of a mile south of that seep there's a strip near the creek about 100 feet wide and 250 feet long that holds about 3 inches of water for several days after a rain. I would run through that water with my combine and never go down more than three or four inches. In the bottom of the ruts was a blue clay so tight you couldn't drive a nail in it with a sledgehammer.

*   *   *   *   *

It seems like mud was always causing trouble for someone. Bobby Laux was cutting wheat one summer on his farm in Callaway County. The ground was pretty soft and once when he pulled up to his truck to unload it looked like it could pour down rain at any minute. Bobby said he knew he needed to tarp the truck and get it out of the field before the ground got any softer, so he backed the combine up and steered to one side to get it out of the way. He said the engine was pulling hard and the wheels were spinning as he backed up, and he thought that the ground must be a lot softer than he realized. When he got out of the combine and saw what he'd done, he thought to himself Bobby, Bobby, Bobby, why in the hell did you do that? He had backed into his pickup and shoved it sideways through the mud for about 6 feet. Bobby told me he had the truck traded off and was just waiting for the new one to come in. He had to put a complete new bedside on his truck to get it back in shape for the trade. It pretty much ruined the straw spreader on the back of the combine, too.

Damn Mud!

My truck at the Murphy Farm. March 1982.

My tractor at the Murphy Farm. March 1982.

Cecil Zumwalt's tractor at the Murphy Farm. March 1982. They all three sat there for a month before we got them out.

*   *   *   *   *

One year I round baled a lot of hay at the Ruggles place that I really didn't need. Sandy Cunningham was short of hay that spring, so I started delivering hay to Sandy twice a week. My trailer hauled four bales at a time, and Sandy said before spring it seemed like every time he looked up "There came Alan with $100 worth of hay." You really don't make much selling big round bales, but it beats the hell out of buying them.

*   *   *   *   *

After Sandy Cunningham passed away I was talking to James Earl Grant one afternoon when he remarked "If things keep going the way they have been for the last couple of years we're not going to have anyone to talk to except each other." It's getting there!

*   *   *   *   *

When I started farming Pappy loaned me his 12-hole John Deere grain drill whenever I needed it. After a couple of years he said there wasn't any reason to wear out the tires pulling it back-and-forth from his farm to mine, and he said for me to keep it at my place. Several years later he told me if he ever needed it again I'd have to use it for him anyhow, so he gave me the drill.

I sowed about a million acres of wheat and soybeans with that little drill before I finally traded it for an 18-hole I. H. drill. David Grant has a three-section folding grain drill, and each section is wider than my whole drill was. I don't know how the hell I ever got anything done.

*   *   *   *   *

In the mid-1970s I traded for a six row 30-inch Ford planter. It was the first six row planter in our neighborhood. After J. R. Jacobs, C. J. Tekotte and Arno Winkler looked it over and had a chance to discuss it, the consensus was "What in the hell does that boy want that great big old clumsy thing for? There's not a gate around here he can get through with it." I did have to saw off a few gate posts, but I got through 'em. I wonder what those three would think if they could see the 15 to 30 row planters that are just average size today.

*   *   *   *   *

For many years before the Watson's purchased it, their farm was known as the Holloway farm. There was a 34-acre field on our farm, just across the fence from Watson's that Pappy and Grandpap always called "The Holloway Ground." During the depression Mr. Holloway was about to lose his farm to the bank. Grandma's mother had just passed away, so Grandma and Grandpap used her inheritance money to buy 34 acres off the Holloway place. This gave Mr. Holloway enough money to pay off his mortgage. The way they decided on 34 acres was because the field that joined the Easley farm surveyed out 34 acres, and that way they didn't have to move any fences.

When I first remember the Holloway ground it had three pretty deep ditches cutting across it. They had grass growing in them, but they were too deep to cross with a tractor. Pappy said Mr. Holloway had "farmed it hard" trying to pay for it. Grandpap and Pappy spent quite a bit of time cutting Cedar brush and throwing it in the ditches, and then Pappy plowed them in the best he could with his 9N Ford and 2-bottom plow. The ditches eventually kind of healed themselves and started growing grass.

In the late 1960s Pappy sold the 34 acres to Perry Phillips and he owned it for over 30 years before selling it along with the rest of his farm for development. It took a couple of days with dozers and big scrapers, but pretty soon those ditches and all of the ridge tops disappeared into a bland, graded off piece of development property. Progress pretty much sucks.

*   *   *   *   *

Owning a farm in a high-traffic area, but not living there, caused Monroe Lanham problems from time to time. He had a 300-gallon gas barrel on his farm at the corner of I 70 and Rangeline Road that he hadn't used for three or four years. He told me that the last time he filled his 8N Ford tractor out of the barrel it ran for less than five minutes before he had to clean the carburetor, blow out all the fuel lines, and remove the sediment bowl from the bottom of the tank and flush the rust and water out of the tank. Since then, the barrel had just sat there with about 18 inches of rusty, watery gas in the bottom.

Early one Sunday morning Mr. Lanham came out to the farm. 100 yards or so before he reached his driveway he noticed an old car sitting at the side of the road with the hood up. When he stopped to open the driveway gate he realized the chain and padlock was missing. He drove up to the house and found the padlock from the gas barrel was missing also.

He called the Sheriff's Department, and after checking things out they had the car towed to the impound lot. When the owner came after it he was arrested for property damage, trespassing and gas theft. And besides all that, his car still wouldn't run because it was full of rusty gas and water. The old boy would've been a lot better off if he'd just stopped at a station and bought a few gallons of gas.

*   *   *   *   *

I rented the Ruggles place on Route Z in 1969 and farmed it for 24 years. Smith & Wesson (Outdoor Brands) recently purchased part of the farm and they have built a humongous distribution center on the property. The area where the house, barn and cattle lots were located is now covered by a 14-acre building. It sure is flatter now than it used to be. Uglier to!

The Ruggles Farm. May 2021.

*   *   *   *   *

In late September 1979, on the first day of fall harvest I started cutting milo on Leroy Sapp's farm. I had cut and unloaded one bin full and was unloading the second one when I smelled smoke. I opened the cab door and stepped out and saw flames reaching 3 to 4 feet above the engine compartment. I grabbed my fire extinguisher, but it had discharged over time and was totally useless. I moved my grain truck so it wouldn't burn too, and then I ran to Leroy's house and called 911.

It didn't take the Boone County Volunteer Fire Department long to get there, but it doesn't take long for a combine to burn up either. Most of my neighbors came to the smoke and we were just standing around watching while the firemen did their thing, when suddenly some idiot headed towards me with his hand outstretched and a big goofy smile on his face. He said "Hi Mr. Easley, I'm whoever with the Columbia Tribune. How are you today?" I looked at him and replied, "That has to be the stupidest god damn question you ever asked in your life!" Then I turned my back on him and walked away. The guy looked at James Earl Grant and asked him if he knew me. When James Earl told him that he did the guy said, "Well that was pretty rude of him, what's his problem?" James Earl said, "Well you ignorant bastard, his combine just burned up, what the hell do you think his problem is?"

The firemen answered the guy's questions, and he got his story, but he damn sure didn't get it from me. Right then I just wasn't in the mood to talk to some idiot!

Cutting beans at Bill Blackwell's with the combine that burned up in 1979.

* * * * *

One afternoon back in the early 1970s Harold Spurgeon was at Jim Nanson's farm south of Arno Winkler's, working on my old 494 John Deere planter. Every time he removed a shaft or sprocket it was slimy/slick with grease. As he wiped the excess grease off of a shaft he remarked "Well, at least it's easier to take apart than the one I worked on down at Hermann last Saturday."

Harold told me that a St. Louis businessman owned a small farm at Hermann and came to the country on weekends to put in a crop. He called Callaway Farmers Equipment Company early one Saturday morning and told them his planter kept breaking chains, so Harold wound up working on the planter in Hermann that Saturday afternoon. He said he had driven three shafts out of the planter with a big hammer and a punch, and had seen nothing but rust flakes and gauld marks. He handed the shafts to the owner and remarked "There's your problem, the planter's burnt up with grease." Harold said the guy looked at him and replied, "Well I don't know why it would be, I've never greased the son of a bitch!"

* * * * *

I pulled Stephen's C Farmall in antique tractor pulls for a year or so after the grandkids got too busy to pull tractors, and I actually finished second behind Bill Blackwell in the 3,250-pound Stock Division one year. However, pulling myself wasn't nearly as much fun as hauling the kids around and watching them pull so the next year the old tractor just sat in the shed. Finally, I mounted an electric powered grass seeder on it and every spring we get it running and sow some clover and lespedeza. A month or so later Greg spreads some fertilizer on his pumpkin patch, then it gets washed and goes back in the shed for another year. You don't see a whole lot of tractors that have wheelie-bars running back and forth across the field, but it works just fine.

*   *   *   *   *

Cattle and walnut logs on the Bearfield farm. December, 2009.

Originally published in Farm Collector, used with permission.

The old place about 5 miles south of Columbia, Missouri, where I was raised has been in the family since the 1840s. The house was built in 1872. According to my mom, the newest building on the farm was built in 1939. Most of the other outbuildings were built before 1900 with logs that were cut on the farm and sawed into lumber on a sawmill that was located in a creek bottom south of the farmstead.

I raised cattle on the place until June 2014, despite the fact that the farm is now surrounded by the city limits of Columbia on three and one-half sides. Great Circle Boys and Girls Town is on the North, a city park with a 40-acre fishing lake is on the East, and a new Catholic high school and homes in the $700,000-800,000 range are on the south. Across the road, a new 66-house subdivision is under construction. A 1/8-mile section of road frontage still connects the farm to non-city property, other than that it is completely surrounded by Columbia. Combine all of that with the fact that the fences I was continuously repairing were the same old fences that I helped repair when I was a kid, and I finally decided it was time to let my cattle go.

Shortly after I sold the cattle, my sister and I entered into negotiations with Boys and Girls Town to sell them 20 acres for a new school and administration building, where the old house and outbuildings were located. Since all of the buildings were to be demolished, I was told that I was welcome to salvage anything that I wanted before the closing date.

There was an old coal shed on the property. It measured 8 feet by 20 feet and had a 12-foot lean-to on the south side. I've been parking tractors in the lean-to since I was old enough to drive one by myself, probably when I was 7 or 8 years old. I decided that I wanted to save the old shed, and since I knew I couldn't handle the project by myself, I called my longtime friend (and some sort of distant cousin), Sandy Cunningham of Cunningham construction.

The old shed, several years before it was moved.

The building originally sat on limestone rocks with a dirt floor. We poured a concrete foundation of the proper size at my place and filled it with gravel. Sandy's crew removed the lean-to, then sawed the main part of the building into sections and hauled them to my place, where the sections were assembled and the lean-to was reattached.

Assembling the old shed at the new location. February 2015.

According to my Grandpap, who was born on the farm in 1862, the coal shed was built in 1875 entirely with rough-sawed oak lumber. Built mostly of pine, the lean-to was apparently added at a later date. The pine didn't last nearly as well as the oak, and all the rafters had to be replaced. Also, the split white oak posts that supported the lean-to had been used up for years, so I cut some good cedar posts off the old farm to replace them. A lot of siding was missing from the lean-to's South wall, so my son Jeff and I salvaged rusty metal roofing from an old hog house to use on that wall. Jeff salvaged oak siding from the old barn on the farm to splice any boards that were rotten on the bottom; most of them were.

The project is now complete and once more there is a tractor parked in the lean-to. Was it economically feasible? Not really, but I wanted to save part of the old place, and this was something I could actually use. The fact that I could have built a new building for less money doesn't really bother me, I'm just glad that I've got the old shed at my place and I'm glad Sandy's crew of Ed and Chris Roberts and John Wright were around to make it happen. They basically made something out of nothing, and now the old shed should be good for at least another 100 years.

The old shed and my Minneapolis Moline M5. July 2015

*   *   *   *   *

I'm 77 and my sister Virginia is a dab older. Neither one of us remembers the old shed ever being anything other than grey, weathered, oak lumber. However, under the eaves where it has been somewhat protected from the weather over the years, you can still see remnants of whitewash. I don't know how many times it was white-washed or when they quit doing it, but at least once in its life, the old shed must have shined like a diamond in a goat's ass.

This picture of the old cellar house was taken in 1906, when it would have been nearly new. It has board and batten siding, the wide boards were painted red, and the narrow bats were painted white. It looks sharp as hell in the picture. I assume the bats were painted white before being nailed on the building, and the first time it was repainted it became solid red and that was the end of the white bats.

Auction sale at the Bearfield Farm, before the short-lived move to California. The new cellar house (upper right) is looking pretty sharp. 1906.

*   *   *   *   *

Whoever coined the phrase Winter Wonderland must have had their head stuck up their butt! On February 15, 2021, after several days of below zero temperatures, the fuel line in my I.H. pick-up froze while the truck was running in the Orscheln Farm and Home parking lot. AAA was apparently overwhelmed by the cold and snow, but I messed with them for a day and a half before arranging my own tow.

While I was waiting at Orscheln for AAA to contact me, Greg called and asked if I had anything that would start. He was on his way to town to get parts for a frozen horse waterer when his truck gelled up. I eventually called AAA and hit the cancel button, then called David Grant to see if I could get a ride home. When he answered I asked what he was up to, and he replied, "I've been working on a frozen waterer, right now I'm setting in the shop watching my truck warm up, hoping it will un-gel so I've got transportation." He had gotten towed earlier in the day. Fran was at the shop with him, so she picked me up and gave me a ride home. It had been snowing since 8:00 a.m. and I hated for her to have to get out, but it sure was appreciated.

Stephen's truck had a wheel bearing going out and he had borrowed my Dakota, so after I got home I started my little Massy loader tractor to bring some more firewood into the garage. It started fine, and after backing out of the shed I made it about 50' before it gelled up and died.

We haven't had a cold spell like this for several years, and we'd gotten complacent. We damn sure weren't ready for it, and it made us look like a bunch of idiots. When the weather is nice I still miss not having cattle, but not when it's like this. Winter Wonder Land my ass!

The Way it Was

When I was growing up there was an odd-shaped White Oak tree at the old place, on the rocky hillside south of the barn where we fed hogs. It was probably 2 feet across from the ground up for about 4 feet, then it pinched in and wasn't over half that big the rest of the way up.

Pappy told me if I ever decided to cut that tree to make sure I sawed at least a foot above the big part. He said that when he and Uncle Edward were kids the tree was hollow about 4 feet up, and had a hole near the top of the hollow part. Pappy said every time they passed the tree they would pick up small flint rocks that would fit through the hole and drop them in, and eventually they got it filled completely. Over the years the hole grew shut, but the tree never got a whole lot bigger.

I haven't seen that old tree for probably 30 years or more, I don't even know if it's still standing or not. I guess I should try to find it, but I probably won't get around to it, I'm awfully ~~busy~~ lazy!

*   *   *   *   *

*Kenneth Jongebloed
and "Dink" the mule. 1941.*

Pappy and Mom got married in 1939. The next summer two of her nephews, Kenneth and Herbert Jongebloed from New York City, came to the farm in Boone County Missouri for summer vacation. Pappy and Mom picked them up at the Greyhound Bus Station in Columbia, and on their way home when Pappy turned off of the gravel road that is now Grindstone Parkway onto the gravel road that is now the paved Bearfield Road, the boys noticed some haystacks near the road on Frank Hall's farm. As they stared eagerly out the window one of the boys asked, "Aunt Margaret, is that where the natives live?"

*   *   *   *   *

Birthday celebration at the Reyburn House. 1904.

Pappy told me that in the late 1800s Will Reyburn decided that he needed a bigger cistern. The Reyburn house was located on a steep ridge above Gans Creek, southeast of where Bearfield Road dead ends, where Charlie Hall's driveway used to be. It is now known as "Wagon Wheel Trailhead."

After Mr. Reyburn and his hired man got the hole dug down several feet, the hired man stayed in the hole and dug while Mr. Reyburn pulled the buckets of dirt and rock to the surface. The ground was dry, hard, and pretty rocky, so the man was doing most of the digging with a pick and a grubbing hoe, just using the shovel to fill the bucket with what he had grubbed out. Once when he made a big swing the pick broke through and a hole about 6 inches across appeared in the bottom of the cistern. He could hear rocks and clods hitting water many feet below. He had apparently broken through the roof of a branch of the Devils Icebox Cave. He came out of that cistern so scared he was shaking, and he refused to go back down. Mr. Reyburn had to go down and get the tools. They covered the hole with a couple of heavy oak planks, then rolled some stumps and big rocks into the cistern before filling it back up. It apparently did a good job of sealing itself, because I walk past the old homesite occasionally, and no sink holes have ever appeared there over the years.

*   *   *   *   *

When you look at those hills, hollers, rocks, bluffs and clay dirt you have to wonder why, after coming all the way from Kentucky in a covered wagon someone would get here and decide this was where they wanted to spend the rest of their life. It must've been a tough S.O.B. where they came from. Either that or their wagon broke down and they just couldn't go any further. Any way you look at it, it was a tough place to make a living. It still is, that's why Rock Bridge Park owns most of it now.

*   *   *   *   *

When I was a kid there wasn't such a thing as weed control chemical, so anything we planted in the cornfield grew, along with all of the weeds that we didn't plant. Grandpap always planted Kentucky Wonder pole beans in the field so they could climb the cornstalks, that was a lot easier than staking them in the garden. Around the edges of the field he also planted lots of pumpkins and the old green and white crook-neck squash. When I can first remember we picked corn by hand (I still have my old shucking peg), and the first couple of loads we picked were always topped off with a pretty good batch of pumpkins and squash.

*   *   *   *   *

Back when I was a kid our family attended Little Bonne Femme Church pretty regularly. I don't remember if the full-time preacher was sick or on vacation, but we had a fill-in preacher for a couple of weeks. After the second sermon Pappy asked one of the older members of the congregation what he thought of the preacher. The old fellow replied "Well, it seems like he uses a lot of words, and it takes him quite a spell to use them, but it just don't seem like he ever says very much." We had a preacher at Olivet Church for a while who must have taken preaching lessons from that feller!

Little Bonne Femme Church. March 2018.

*   *   *   *   *

When I was growing up we always had some sort of a neighborhood ball team. Me, Kenny and John Cavcey, Tom and Jim Watson, Tommy Stewart, Leroy

Dirksmeyer, Andy and Jackie Rule and anyone else who came by and wanted to play. If we could get a game going with some guys from another neighborhood we would, if not we'd choose up sides and play among ourselves. We really didn't care we just liked to play. Sometimes when we chose sides we'd be so shorthanded that the same three outfielders played for both teams.

One afternoon we were playing a bunch of boys from around the big town of Harg. John Cavcey was playing second base, and about halfway through the game Don Gibson slid into second and spiked the hell out of him. That pretty much ended the game, the grown-ups took John to the emergency room, and the rest of us tagged along to see if he was going to bleed to death. Another time we were playing the same team and Dean Powell hit me in the head with a pitch. RANG MY BELL! Those boys were damn near to mean for us to be playing with.

*   *   *   *   *

Uncle Paul Cheavens told me that when he and Aunt Susie got married in 1917 he wanted Susie to know that she had married a good provider, so that fall he went to a neighbor's and purchased 5 gallons of sorghum molasses. He didn't realize that a quart of sorghum will go a long ways, much less 5 gallons!

I 'spect Aunt Susie was gouging out sorghum crystals and heating them up to re-liquefy them for several years. Anyhow, Uncle Paul said that was the only time he ever bought 5 gallons of sorghum molasses.

*   *   *   *   *

When I was a little kid I loved to listen to Grandpap tell stories, unless he was just talking about old times then my mind tended to wander a little. He said that for a while a young man lived with them who was an epileptic. I didn't bother asking if he was some kind of kin, or if he worked on the farm or if he just boarded there, it didn't really seem very important at the time.

Anyhow, Grandpap said one night the man had an epileptic fit. The temperature was close to zero, and Grandpap said as he ran out of the house to saddle a horse and ride to town to get the doctor, the hat he grabbed by mistake didn't have ear flaps. By the time he rode 8 miles to the doctor's house and 8 miles back, his ears were frozen solid. The doctor told his mother to have someone hold hands full of snow over his ears so they would thaw out slow. He said most of the skin peeled off of his ears but other than that they never gave any problems, so apparently the snow worked. I guess the guy lived through his fit, but I didn't bother to ask. I really don't know what the hell I was thinking about. Or not thinking about.

*   *   *   *   *

There's no doubt that when DDT was first invented it was way overused and it did a bunch of long-term damage over the years. There's also no doubt that when it went on the market it was pretty much the answer to a lot of prayers. Pappy told me that when he was young man anytime there was a large meal, whether a family reunion, threshing or whatever, one or two of the women wouldn't eat 'til everyone else was finished. It was their job to walk around the table with fans and keep the air stirred up enough that the flies wouldn't land on the food dishes. Now if one or two flies get in the house we're aggravated because we have to chase them down and swat them.

*   *   *   *   *

When I was a kid no one had air conditioners, so the windows and doors were always open in hot weather. When we went in or out of the house we would slap the screen door with our hand to scare off the flies, so they wouldn't swarm in when the door was opened.

Whenever we finished a meal Mom or Grandma always did the dishes immediately. Instead of being put away in the cabinet they would be stacked in the middle of the table and covered with a tea towel, to keep the flies off them 'til the next meal. Once when I was a pretty little squirt Momma walked into the kitchen one afternoon, then in a very shocked tone of voice said, "Alan look at all of those flies!" I said, "Don't worry, Momma, they're all dead." I had been swatting flies all afternoon, then carefully picking them up and placing them on the table and on the towel, there were probably over 100 dead flies laying there.

The dish stacks were different heights, so the towel draped over them made a perfect mountain range where my Indian flies could hide. The ones on the surface of the table were my Soldier flies, coming to shoot those common, no account Indian flies. For some reason Momma was extremely un-impressed with my little game; I never played that little game again.

*   *   *   *   *

The invention of rat and mouse poison was another thing that made life easier on the farm. The old house on Bearfield Road wasn't rodent proof, it had holes and cracks that just kept on getting bigger over the years, so we kept a few mouse traps set at all times, but the rats had been pretty much poisoned out of existence by when I can first remember.

Pappy said when he and Uncle Edward were growing up, on rainy afternoons they would take their .22 rifles and go to the barn and shoot rats. He said it wasn't at all unusual to kill 25 or 30 rats in an afternoon, and sometimes even more. I'm glad they're not that thick now, there's just something about a damn rat that I really don't like!

*   *   *   *   *

There's some really good farm ground surrounding the town of Centralia. However, Pappy told me that when he was a young man if someone mentioned that they farmed near Centralia everyone felt a little bit sorry for them. Pappy said that the flat ground up there was sour, and there were big areas that were so wet that most years they couldn't be farmed. In the 1940s farmers started spreading a lot of lime and sweetening the soil, and installing drain tile in the bolly-wogs. It's a lot better ground now than the hills around Columbia that I'm used to farming. It just needed a bunch of TLC.

*   *   *   *   *

As long as I can remember, in the early spring when the frost went out of the ground and it was too muddy to do anything else, Pappy would drive around the pastures dragging a log chain behind the tractor. When he'd see a thorn sprout or Cedar tree big enough that the chain would stay hooked, he'd stop and hitch on, then pull the sprout out by the roots and drag it to the nearest ditch. If I had continued that practice the old place would look a hell of a lot better than it does now!

*   *   *   *   *

One spring in the late 1970s Pappy was on one of his sprout-pulling missions. He was on the hillside east of

Clear Creek when he spotted a thorn about the right size. He stopped and got off, picked up the end of the chain and prepared to hook onto the sprout. He said "Alan, by the time I got to the tree the chain wouldn't reach it!"

He looked at the tractor and it was slowly rolling downhill toward the creek. There was a 6-inch diameter Cedar tree between the tractor and the creek, and Pappy said he was hoping it would miss the tree, until he realized that if his tractor went over the creek bank it would land on its nose and probably flip upside down. Then he started rooting for the tree.

The right front wheel went just outside of the tree, the axle hit it and the tractor came to a halt. Pappy crippled the tractor back to the house with that one front wheel towed in so much it was pretty much sliding sideways instead of rolling. Like all Fords, the 860 had a two-piece axle on each side so the wheels could be set wider for cultivating. The inner section of the axle had a right smart of a bend in it, and the end of it was jammed against the radiator drain plug. Pappy called A. F. Fullington, and he came out the next day to survey the damage. He told Pappy he could remove the axle and take it to a machine shop and have it pressed straight. Then he said if Pappy never intended to spread the wheels that there was a cheaper way. Pappy told him to go to the cheaper route, so A. F. reached in with a cutting torch and cut about 2 inches off the axle where it was pressed against the drain plug, then he adjusted the drag links so that the wheels ran straight.

When Pappy died in 1982 the tractor still had that bent axle. Bill Blackwell bought the tractor at Pappy's auction, and used it 'til he died in 2016, and his son Randy still has it. Randy knows that if he ever decides to sell the 860 I want to be the new owner. If I do get the old tractor back someday that axle is gonna stay just like it is.

It's been that way for 40 years, and there's no use fixing it now.

*   *   *   *   *

Marcia always liked to use rocks in her flowerbeds, and Pappy was always on the lookout for ones she could use. One rock that she hauled home from the old place was a slab of limestone 4 inches thick, 18 inches wide at the backend and 14 inches wide in the front, with a 5/8" hole drilled through the narrow end. Naturally the hole had been drilled by hand, with a hammer and star drill, and the rock was shaped with a hammer and a chisel. Pappy told Marcia it was a "corn rock." He said after their corn got to tall to cultivate, they drug the rock between the corn rows with a small horse or mule, to knock out little weeds when they first came up. That took a while, one row middle at a time. Now a custom applicator unfolds 75- or 100-foot booms, and does more in an afternoon than one man, with a mule and that rock could've done all summer.

*   *   *   *   *

In 2015, before Great Circle Boys and Girls Town demolished the big barn on the old farm, Jeff was salvaging some 12-inch_to 18-inch-wide White Oak planks, some of them 20 feet long. In the south end of the barn there were two grain bins, floored with white oak planks with 3/8 X 3" strips nailed over the cracks between the planks. In the center of the west bin there was a stack of limestone rocks supporting the center beam. Under the east bin the stack of rocks was topped with an old cast-iron gear that had three teeth stripped off. People today think they invented recycling, but that old barn was built in 1874; the builders were way ahead of their time. They probably didn't even realize that they were recycling, they just used the gear because it fit, and it saved them the trouble of looking for the right size rock.

Bill Blackwell sandblasting the old gear that Jeff found under the barn.

The old gear, sandblasted, painted, and sitting in the way on my front porch.

*   *   *   *   *

Pappy said one afternoon when he and Uncle Edward were in their teens they were "projectin' around" on the bluff face south of Dry Cave. At that time it would've been on the Reyburn place, later it belonged to Charlie Hall, and it is now part of Rock Bridge State Park.

Pappy said somewhere on that bluff face they discovered an extremely old American Flag chiseled into the limestone. He said they didn't make any special effort to mark the spot because they had no doubt that they could find it whenever they wanted to, but they were wrong. They looked several times over the years, but they never found it again.

Tommy Stewart told me that he and Tom Watson found someone's initials and the date chiseled into the bluff in the same general area. He doesn't remember the initials or the date, and they never located them again. It's been over 100 years since Pappy and Uncle Edward saw the flag, and probably 60 years since Tommy saw the initials and I'm sure that they have weathered a lot during that time, but it might be interesting if the Park had some of their interns crawl around on that bluff face, just to see what they could find.

*   *   *   *   *

Momma always cooked a big meal whenever there was a hay crew or whatever working at the farm, but she eventually decided she'd cooked all she ever wanted to cook. For several years after Pappy died one of the boys and I would mow hay on the old place, then David Grant, Randy Blackwell, Greg, Jeff or maybe Kevin Brown would rake while James Earl rolled up big bales and I started moving them out of the field. There were always three people, and sometimes four there at mealtime. Mom would fix fried chicken, pork chops or roast beef with all the trimmings, and usually cake or cookies for dessert.

One day after we finished eating David Grant said "Mrs. Easley, that was a really good meal." Momma was never bashful, she always said exactly what was on her mind, and she replied "Well I'm glad you liked it David, because that's the last one you're ever getting. I've cooked my last big meal, next year you all are on your own."

She meant it, not only was that the last big meal she ever cooked, but it was also almost the last meal of any size she ever cooked. She'd get the skillet out and fry a little bacon and some eggs for breakfast, but other than that she pretty much got by on Meals on Wheels and

Stouffer's "Hungry Man" dinners. She'd heat one of those in the oven for dinner and have enough left over to microwave for supper. When I'd take her to the store she'd buy two dozen of those things at a time. She still loved a good steak, and when Marcia and I would take her out for supper she would eat like a field hand, but she didn't want good food bad enough to fix it for herself.

*　　*　　*　　*　　*

When Momma finally had to go to a Nursing Home at the age of 96 she had congestive heart failure, and an aneurysm in her chest the size of a tennis ball. She also had a prediabetic condition, and some "by the book" dietitian put her on a sugar-free diet. When I asked why, I was told they didn't want her to develop diabetes. I kind of came un-glued, and said "Ma'am, she's 96 years old, she's not going to live long enough to develop diabetes, she knows that she came here to die, why don't you let her eat what she wants, what the hell difference could it possibly make?" Apparently it made a lot of difference to them, because they kept her on that sugar-free diet.

I never knew a time when Momma didn't have a carton of Hershey Bars in the house, and after about a week of sugar-free dessert she said "Alan, I really think I'm going to need some Hershey Bars." When I asked plain or with almonds she replied, "A box of each would be nice." She ate at least one Hershey Bar after supper every day she was in the Home, plus at least once a week Marcia would take her half a pie cut into two pieces. She would eat one piece as soon as it arrived and eat the other piece the next morning before breakfast. One morning Mom was sitting up in bed happily eating a quarter of a pecan pie when a nurse walked in and told her she wasn't supposed to be eating pecan pie. Mom looked at her and said, "Do you REALLY think you can take it away from me?" She finished her pie with no further interruptions.

Mom lived less than a year after she went to the Home, and I like to think that those Hershey Bars and pie made the time a little more bearable.

*   *   *   *   *

The Christmas before Grindstone School burned John Cavcey and I shared the janitor's job. When classes were out for the holidays John and I went to the school on alternate days to stoke the fire. We would start it and let it burn hard for an hour or so to warm the building, then when it had burned down to coals we'd stuff enough coal in the furnace to keep fire most of the night. While we were waiting we did some mopping, waxing, etc., that we were expected to get done before school opened again. One day when I walked to the school there was 3 or 4 inches of snow on Bearfield Road. Grindstone Road had been graded but it had about 1 inch of hard packed snow on it. Before I finished my chores it had come a light freezing drizzle.

When the rain started Pappy decided to come pick me up with his 860 Ford tractor that he had bought about six weeks earlier. It was 20 minutes or so after he got there before I was ready to leave and by the time we got on the tractor and headed home the freezing drizzle had turned that snow packed road into a skating rink. Pappy never drove a tractor over half throttle when it was in road gear, so we headed west just puttering along. We got down the first little hill and halfway up the next one before the tractor spun out. Pappy backed up as far as he could and took off a little faster, with the same results. He backed up again and took off at full throttle. We made it about three quarters of the way up before sideslipping and spinning out again. Long about this time a car came by heading west, with tire chains on. We'd never seen the guy before, but he stopped and said if we had a chain he'd pull us to the top of the hill. It was an easy pull, and after we un-hooked Pappy offered to pay him but he said no, he was just glad to help. As soon as we turned south on Bearfield Road Pappy said "Alan, I'm sure glad Raymond Myers didn't see that car pulling my Ford tractor up the hill, he never would've let me forget it."

*   *   *   *   *

It didn't matter how good Pappy's tractor was, Raymond's was always just a little bit better. Actually, it didn't matter if it was a tractor, truck, cow or a new hat, Raymond would look at whatever you had and say "By God, that's a pretty good one, but I've got one at home that's better." Raymond had a 315 I. H. combine, and when I bought my 303 I. H. he said, "By God, I don't know why you bought that thing when you could've got one like mine."

I asked a mechanic who worked for the I.H. Dealer what the difference was between a 315 and a 303. He replied, "Well, the 303 is a pretty good little combine, and the 315 is International's version of an Edsel!"

Ford didn't just build the Edsel; they also built the 620 combine. The 630 and the 640 Fords were pretty good combines, but the 620 was definitely an Edsel!

*   *   *   *   *

Before Stephen's old Bassett Hound Cloe passed away, she did most of her sleeping in the family room. The carpet wasn't soft enough to suit her, so I always kept two heavy lined flannel shirts on the floor for her bed. She slept in front of the entertainment center, and at the corner of it next to her bed was a 2-foot-tall heavy plastic

Santa Clause. For a Santa he was pretty skinny. Cloe never paid any attention to the Santa, occasionally when she rolled over she would bump him a little, but other than that she just ignored him. One evening she rolled over in her sleep and bumped him pretty hard, he rocked back-and-forth a couple of times then fell and landed on her. Cloe yipped and yarped like she'd been beat with a club. My daughter-in-law Jamie had commented several times about what a neat Santa that was, so when she and Greg got home from work the next day I took it over and gave it to her.

The next time Cloe walked over to her little nest she sniffed the carpet where the Santa had been, then she laid down and whimpered and whined for at least five minutes before she went to sleep. She did this every time she went to her bed for the next couple of days. Finally, Stephen went to the storage room and found another Santa and put it were the first one had been. This one was about half as tall as the original, and a whole bunch fatter. The next time Cloe came in she walked over and sniffed him real good, then laid down, let out a big sigh and went to sleep. She didn't care how tall he was, she just wanted a Santa by her bed to keep her company.

* * * * *

I've known Jack Blaylock forever and I consider him to be one of the best appraisers to ever work in Boone County. However, in the early 80s we got plumb crossways once. Jack called me and said the City of Columbia had hired him to appraise the right-of-way for the proposed sewer line, so that they could make their initial cheap assed offer. I told him I had cattle on the farm but they shouldn't be any problem.

They wouldn't of been if Jack had shut the damn gate, but it was in the upper 90s the day he came out and he didn't expect the cattle to be moving around, so he left it open. Momma called me later that day and she was so breathless she couldn't hardly talk. She told me someone had left the gate open and the cows got out, and that her and Gladys Cavcey had spent 1½ hours walking them slowly back down the road.

I called Jack at home and asked him if he had appraised the right-of-way on Mom's that afternoon, and if he had left the gate open while he was there. When he answered yes to both questions I said "Jack, you stupid piece of shit!" I told him that two 75-year-old women were out in the heat for 1 1/2 hours getting the cows back in, it was a good thing neither of them had a heart attack or stroke in the heat, he was a sorry worthless bastard and he was going to pay them $75 each for their time, he was a really dumb son of a bitch, and I just kept on 'til I finally ran out of breath. Jack apologized, I accepted, and we pretty much forgot about it.

When Momma died in 2006 I needed an appraisal on the farm for Estate Tax purposes. I stopped by Jack's office to see if he could do one for me. He said he'd come out the next week, and as I started to leave I said "Jack, shut the gate while you're there or you might get a cussing." He kind of smiled and replied, "In my line of work you get lots of cussings, but some of them stick with you a little longer than others."

*   *   *   *   *

When the boys were in kindergarten/1st grade at New Haven School they brought a note home one afternoon about a Parenting Class that was going to be held at the school the next Friday night. We had no idea what it was about, but we decided to go and find out.

When the class started it soon became apparent that the instructor didn't believe in our style of parenting, and we quickly realized that no one there except us had ever considered spanking a child. Except for us everyone there, including the instructor, believed in letting the kids run the circus.

The longer the class went on, the more dis-interested we got. Several times Marcia looked at me, rolled her eyes and kind of smiled. Finally, the instructor told us what should be done if a small child was standing up in a rocking chair, and vigorously rocking back-and-forth. She said you should gently stop the chair from rocking and explain to the child that this behavior could cause them to get hurt, that you didn't want that to happen, and you would really appreciate it if they would stop. She said if they persisted you should gently lift them from the chair and again explain to them how dangerous it was for them to do this.

Marcia was wearing her eyes out as she'd glance at me and roll them while gently shaking her head. Finally, the instructor asked if anyone would handle the situation differently. I said "Yes Ma'am, I would. The first time I'd say 'Boy, sit down and quit rocking like that right now.' If he didn't sit down I'd say 'Boy, this is the second time I've told you to quit. I won't tell you again, I'll just twist your arm off at the elbow and beat you to death with it!'" There were several gasps of horror, and the instructor just stood there with a shocked expression on her face. Marcia looked at me and said, "We're done here, aren't we?" I nodded, and after we walked out to dead silence she remarked "We might've found something to do that would've been a bigger waste of time, but I really can't imagine what it would've been." The instructor must of thought we were a waste of time too, cause I guaran-damn-tee we never got invited to anymore Parenting Classes.

*   *   *   *   *

The columns at Eighth and Walnut in Columbia, from the old Boone County Courthouse that was demolished in 1909, have a stair step base and have had for many years. However, when I was a kid the base of the columns had a flat ledge about 18 inches wide, probably 3 feet or so above the ground. In decent weather by 9 o'clock the bums and winos would be perched on the columns, sipping from their gin, vodka or wine bottles and asking for handouts. They would sit there and drink 'til they passed out, going into the Courthouse (no security check) to use the public restroom whenever necessary, and making lewd, crude comments to any women who had to pass that way alone. It finally got so bad that the County hired a contractor to rebuild the base of the columns so the drunks could no longer sit there. I guaran-damn-tee that the women didn't think that happened any too soon.

Old Friends and Neighbors

Years ago, I was attending a farm auction south of Columbia. Bob Baumgartner had just bought a hotdog at the food booth and unwrapped one end of it. Before he could take a bite someone walked up and started talking to him, and he was just standing there holding that hot dog at his side. I opened my pocketknife, walked up beside Bob, took hold of the unwrapped end of the hot dog and sliced it off flush with his hand. As I walked away I said, "Thank you, Bob, I was a little hungry, this ought to take care of it." That was over 20 years ago, and Bob still mentions that hotdog occasionally. He says he intends to collect for it someday when conditions are just right.

I don't see Bob nearly as often as I used to. A few years ago he bought a farm south of Belle, Missouri, and moved away from his home place south of me. He said there are a lot more rocks down there, but a lot fewer idiots. It sounds to me like he made a pretty good trade.

* * * * *

I ran into Velda Davison at Westlake's Hardware in November 2017, and we blocked the aisle and made people go around us for 30 minutes or more as we talked old times. I hadn't seen Velda since Tom's funeral. Back when they lived just west of us we used to visit back and forth all the time. When I was moving machinery from one farm to another, Tom and his old dog Freckle hauled me around lots of times over the years. I always thought Bassett Hounds had short legs until I met Freckle. His legs were just barely long enough to reach the ground.

Me moving a little grain bin. Mid-1980s.

*   *   *   *   *

One evening I was sitting with Charlie and Carol Lee, Ronnie, Janice and Dolores McCray, Steve and Peggy Whipple and Wayne and Jo Behymer at a turkey supper at Oakland Church. It looked kind of like an Olivet Church reunion. As usual I was wearing a pair of bib overalls and a red plaid shirt. Someone remarked that Marca had spent over 50 years civilizing me, but the veneer must've been pretty damn thin. I had to agree with them.

For many years, five minutes before Marcia and I were ready to walk out the door to go somewhere she would look at me and ask "Alan, you really weren't intending to wear those overalls, were you?" I'd reply, "Of course not Babe, I'm just waiting 'til the last minute to put on my jeans, because I don't want them to get wrinkled." I never did make it out of the door in my overalls, but I sure do now.

*   *   *   *   *

One summer back in the late 1970s Marcia and I went to the State Fair in Sedalia with Bill and Doris Blackwell and stayed for two or three days in their camper. Doris's sister and brother-in-law, Donna and Jack Hall, met us there and we had a lot of fun wandering around looking at the exhibits, drinking a little beer and attending a couple of country music concerts.

Bill, Jack, Doris and Donna were all raised in the Missouri Bootheel, in the Naylor/Poplar Bluff area. There was a Bluegrass band playing at the Beer Garden that year and any time we got close Jack would tip the band a couple of dollars to play 40 Miles to Poplar Bluff. There were a couple of kids singing with the band who were pretty good entertainers.

When I went to Doniphan Missouri for Bill's funeral in November 2016, Randy, Beverly and I were visiting at Jack and Donna's the morning of the service. Somehow the conversation made it around to the Beer Garden band. Donna asked me if I remembered who the kids were who sang with the band. When I told her that I never did know, she told me it was the Saliegh Mountain Band playing, and the kids were Rhonda and Darren Vincent, now performing with the groups Rhonda Vincent and the Rage, and Dailey and Vincent, two of the hottest Bluegrass acts around today. If I'd have known those kids were going to get that famous I'd probably have paid a little more attention to them.

*   *   *   *   *

In September 2017 I attended the Heritage Festival which is held at Nifong Park and the Boone County Historical Society Museum. Richard Sorrels had his 1914 International truck on display, and I had my 1950 Dodge pickup. We were parked across from the Easley Store building, which had been moved from Easley, Missouri, on the banks of the Missouri River. Richard and I were sitting in lawn chairs, visiting and watching the crowd. A lady walked up and said "Mr. Easley, you probably don't remember me, I'm Jennifer Jones Lehman, John and Joyce Jones daughter". Then she said, "You taught me how to make mint juleps at the Olivet Church Bar-B-Que one year when I was in Junior High School, and I still remember how to make them." I told her there were several women who attended Olivet who weren't really happy about the mint juleps, beer, and kids at a Church Bar-B-Que, but they eventually got over it.

*   *   *   *   *

Gary Chandler is a right decent finish carpenter. He can build cabinets, furniture, or whatever else you might need. Back in the late 1960s he helped me build a 24' x 36' hay shed southwest of the house. I built it with Black Locust and Catalpa poles, some not real straight, and all used lumber, some Oak and some Pine, not all the same dimensions. The sides were covered with used tin, some corrugated, some the old wide corrugated, and some the really old standing rib. Gary wasn't real proud of my choice of building materials, and he never did get used to me cutting rafters with a chainsaw and trimming them to fit with a hatchet, but it worked and the old shed is still standing.

I've stored a lot of square bales in it over the years and it has 50 or 75 bales in it now for Leah's horses, plus a pile of Oak lumber and a couple of old tractors that need to be restored, so it's still serving its purpose. I paint it every few years, and from the road it looks about as good as any other hay shed. Not bad for less than a $300 investment.

The old hay shed.

*   *   *   *   *

Recently I ran into Jim Lee, Charlie and Carol's son, at an auction in Centralia. It had probably been 40 years since I'd seen him. He looked vaguely familiar but I couldn't place him, the only reason that he knew me is that the back of my coat said, "Easley Family Farm." We talked about when he and his brother John used to come out to the house with Charlie and Carol on Sunday afternoons, and how they would roam the whole farm with Greg and Jeff and not come back to the house 'til they were hungry. Life was a lot simpler back then. Now people are afraid to let kids out of their sight and I guess there are some good reasons for that, but it seems like kids were a lot better off when they could play outside on their own, instead of making blisters on their thumbs playing some dumb ass computer game. That was my social commentary for the day, I'm done now.

*   *   *   *   *

T.B. Stewart and sheep. 1958.

Jimmy Stewart passed away recently. The day of his visitation I got to thinking about when T.B. and Julia built their house on Bearfield Road, south of Doc and Hattie Fortney's place. It was the mid-1950s, and a couple of those years were hot, dry son-of-a-bitches.

Not long after they moved in, T. B. decided the boys needed a flock of sheep to care for. They soon wound up with 15 ewes, which would have been just about right most years, but the old farm had been kind of neglected before T.B. bought it, and when it quit raining and the temperatures started hitting 100 degrees every day it wasn't long before the grazing was gone.

Jim and Tom were able to buy a little hay locally, but no one really wanted to sell any, because everyone had to start feeding early. The ASCS, now known as the Farm Service Agency, declared Boone County a disaster area and started shipping in western hay on the railroad, and selling it to local farmers at a discounted price. However, they couldn't get in as much at a time as was needed, so the hay was dispensed in the order that farmers had signed up. The boys were out of feed and were still quite a ways down on the list, so T.B. brought them up to see Pappy and Grandpap with a proposition. They wanted to borrow hay from Pappy and Grandpap, then replace it when their hay came in. We had hay on hand, so the arrangements were made. T. B. had an old 1947 Ford pickup and every weekend he would bring the boys to the farm so they could load enough hay to last for a week. Eventually their hay came in, and they replaced the borrowed hay before hauling the rest of it down the road to T. B.'s farm. It worked out O.K. for everyone, and the sheep made it through the summer.

Jimmy Stewart and sheep. Mid-1950s.

*   *   *   *   *

Years ago, James Earl Grant was over at the house one afternoon and somehow during the conversation he mentioned that he needed a front tractor tire. I don't remember why it was there, but I had a pretty decent used tire laying in the shed. I said something about needing a tire for the dummy axle on my grain truck and James Earl said that he had one, so we decided to swap tires. The only problem was that was that his truck tire was in town at Como Tire Supply where he had left it when he got a new tire put on the front of his grain truck, so we climbed in his pickup and headed for Como's.

When we got there James Earl told Rusty Coats that he had come to pick up his truck tire. Rusty went to the warehouse and before long he returned and told James Earl that he didn't have a tire there. James Earl reminded him that when he bought the new tire for his grain truck that Rusty had told him there was no hurry, just pick up the old tire whenever it suited. Rusty said "James Earl, you need to store your own tires, I don't have room to store tires for every farmer in Boone County." I saw James Earl's fist starting to close and his arm starting to draw back, so I hooked my arm around his and said "Easy, easy, easy." He relaxed and nobody got hit, but that smart remark cost Como Tire most of James Earl's business for several years.

*   *   *   *   *

After Pappy passed away Momma lived on the farm by herself for 25 years before finally going to a Nursing Home at the age of 96. She made it fine for a long time, but like the old house along toward the end she was deteriorating pretty fast. She didn't see well at all, and she was almost deaf.

Bucky Roberts called me one afternoon around 6 o'clock and his voice had a quiver in it when he told me that he had almost run over Mom with his truck. He had been working on a little job in Bearfield Subdivision south of Mom's house; he was on his way home and as he came up the hill he saw Momma at her mailbox. When he was almost there she turned and walked across the road without looking. Bucky slammed on his brakes and hit the ditch, and he said Momma just kept on walking, she didn't even realize anything had happened. Bucky probably wasn't running over 30 mph, it's a good thing it was him instead of some of the idiots who drove that road like it was I-70.

*   *   *   *   *

On December 26, 2017, I ran into Frank and John Glenn at MFA in Columbia. John told me he had enjoyed my second book, and said he was surprised I didn't mention the time that Irl Brooks thought John and I were trying to kill each other. I'd kind of forgotten about that, but it came back to me pretty quick after he reminded me.

My old orange grain truck was sitting on the scales at MFA with a load of wheat one afternoon when John pulled away from the dump pit and stopped at the scales, heading out. He walked into the office, looked at me and said, "I'm in a hurry, get that sorry piece of shit out of my way, you damned old sow bellied slut!" I replied, "You can kiss my ass, you fat bastard," and then we grabbed each other and went to the floor. We were rolling around stirring up a lot of dust, cussing each other, kicking stuff off the shelves and having a hell of a good old time when Irl came running out of his office, prepared to do whatever was necessary to keep someone from getting seriously hurt. When he finally realized we were just playing he said he'd hate to hear what we'd call each other if we were actually mad.

*   *   *   *   *

Back in the late 1960s I was helping Gary Chandler remodel the house in Centralia where he and Lynn lived. Gary didn't usually borrow a lot of stuff from his father-in-law, Verle Coolley, but we were generating lots of lathe and plaster, junk pipe, scrap lumber and some old plumbing fixtures, so Gary borrowed Verle's new Chevy pickup to haul the stuff to the trash hollow on the back side of Verle's farm.

Gary backed in pretty close to the edge of the ditch and we drug everything off of the truck, then he tossed about half a pint of charcoal lighter on the scrap pile, lit it, and then we climbed in the truck to leave but we didn't go anywhere. It was a 2 WD truck, and it spun once and settled itself about 6 inches into the soft ground. We didn't have a shovel with us, so we grabbed some 2x4s out of the ditch and used them to gouge around in the mud in front of the wheels. I got behind the truck and pushed and Gary stomped his foot to the floor and eventually pulled away from the pile. He stopped and got out, and with a look of relief on his face he commented "Damn that was close." I looked at the back of the truck and said, "A little bit too damn close if you ask me!" The pickup had plastic taillight lenses, and the left-hand lens had gotten way too hot. It was still there, but the plastic had slumped down in waves and looked like a snowman on a warm day. Gary never did tell me how he explained that lens to Verle, but I'd bet it was an interesting conversation.

*   *   *   *   *

I was fooling around out by my machine shed one afternoon when an SUV pulled in off the road and stopped. It was Harry and Charlene Smith, who I have known probably forever. Harry was one of the youngest of a whole flock of Smith kids. I went to school with some of his older brothers and Greg and Jeff went to school with Harry.

We talked for at least an hour, and somewhere during that time we got on the subject of school buses. The bus didn't go down the dead-end road to Herman Smith's house, it stopped on Bass Lane west of David Allen's house and the Smith kids walked a quarter of a mile or so to reach it. Raymond Hendricks was the bus driver, and usually a couple of times a week the kids wouldn't be there when the bus stopped. At that time the bus was required (by state law) to wait one minute if the kids weren't at the pickup point. However, if they were in sight it had to wait 'til they arrived. Raymond would sit there checking his watch and usually just as he was ready to leave three or four kids would top the hill, running as hard as they could. After they were in sight it was still an eighth of a mile or so to the bus, and as soon as they could be seen they would slow to a walk. Raymond would sit there mumbling under his breath, and by the time the kids reached the bus you could almost see steam coming out of his ears, but there wasn't anything he could do about it, and it wouldn't be but a few days until it would happen again.

*   *   *   *   *

Bob Dudley is one of the last of the old-school barbers around. When you go to Bob you don't just get a haircut; he trims your eyebrows, clips the hair out of your ears, tells a few stories, shaves your neck and if you've got any moles that look different than they did the last time you were there he'll tell you to go get them checked.

The only problem is, by the time Bob and Nonie spend the winter in Florida, and Bob goes to South Dakota, Nebraska and Iowa pheasant hunting, and then hunts mushrooms, deer and quail in Boone County, that doesn't leave but about three weeks out of the year when he has time to cut hair. Bob said you have to take care of the important things first.

*   *   *   *   *

Bob Dudley and I go to the same Dermatologist. I recently had a pre-cancerous thing frozen off my ear. When the doctor first walked into the exam room he asked what was going on with my ear. I told him I didn't know for sure because Dudley was still in Florida, and the little gal at the clip joint where I got my last haircut wasn't nearly as concerned with my ears as Bob is.

He said, "I'll bet she was better looking than Bob." I replied, "She could be a pretty damn ugly woman and still be better looking than Bob." He laughed and said "Well _____ ____ _____;" Bob, I'm not going to tell you what he said, you'll have to ask him yourself, the next time you see him.

*   *   *   *   *

Monroe Lanham was never actually a neighbor, but I rented his farm for close to 20 years and I always considered him a friend. The little house on his farm at the corner of I-70 and Rangeline Road was furnished well enough that when he came out on weekends he could be comfortable. One really nice item of furniture in the house was a glass front China Cabinet. One Sunday morning when Mr. Lanham stopped to unlock the driveway gate he saw tire tracks in the snow outside the gate. Inside the gate he noticed two sets of footprints going in, and two sets coming back out. When he got to the house he realized that the padlock had been prized off the back door. When he went inside he saw all the dishes from the China Cabinet scattered around on the kitchen table and chairs, but the cabinet itself was nowhere to be seen.

The sheriff's department came out and looked things over, then took a detailed description of the cabinet. About two months later it showed up in an antique furniture consignment auction. Mr. Lanham got his China Cabinet back and considering the fact that it had been carried 200 yards down a snowy driveway, lifted over the top of a metal gate, hauled somewhere and stored for two months and then hauled to an auction, it was still in really good condition. A couple of pretty much local boys did a hell of a lot of work for nothing. All they had to show for all that work was probation.

Just Neighbors

Eutsy Johnson and I never did see eye to eye on most things, but one year in early September he called me and wanted to buy 1000 bales of horse hay. I had some beautiful Timothy and Alsike Clover that I had baled on Brian Mitchell's place, and I priced it to Eutsy for $2.50 per bale delivered. He grunted and said there was no way he would pay that much for hay, and then he offered me a $1.50 per bale. I told him I wouldn't take that for good hay, but if he wanted cheap hay I had some I'd deliver for $1.00 per bale. He didn't even ask what kind it was, he just told me where to unload.

I had around 1200 bales of stubble clover mowed down but not baled yet. The straw had laid in the field long enough that it was pretty weathered and the mixed weeds were as tall as the new clover. It was pretty damn common stuff and I was just baling it so the hay would be clean the next year. I'd been hoping I could find a landscaper needing some cheap mulch, so I was tickled to death to find a place to get rid of it right out of the field.

I got it baled and then my hippie hay haulers delivered 1000 bales to Eutsy. He paid me and that was the last I heard from him 'til late the next spring. I was checking fence one afternoon between the Murphy place and Eutsy's, when he drove up on his side and got out. He didn't waste any time on preliminaries, he walked over to the fence and said "Easley, that hay you sold me last fall was worthless!" When I asked him what was wrong with it he said, "My horses wouldn't touch that stuff, did your cows eat it?" I replied, "They probably would have if they'd got hungry enough, but I had plenty of good hay so I didn't even try to make them eat that crap." Eutsy grunted and walked away, and as far as I can remember that was the last time he and I ever spoke.

*   *   *   *   *

Pappy was on the school board back in the early 1950s, when the seven one-room country schools were trying to merge and build what would be known as New Haven R II. A site had been purchased for the school about 3 miles east of where it finally got built. Charlie and Gussie Trimble, who lived several miles southeast of our farm, wanted the school built further south. Actually, they wanted it built on a farm that they owned west of the TV station.

The bond issue had already been voted down two or three times, and as the School Board prepared for another vote the rumors, distortions and flat-assed lies were spreading like wildfire. Momma always was kind of blunt, but she was usually pretty mild-mannered unless you started telling lies about Pappy, then she got pissed off real quick. One afternoon someone knocked on the door and when Momma answered it was Gussie Trimble, looking for Pappy. Momma said, "He's out at the barn, if you want to talk to him go find him!" And then she slammed the door in Gussie's face. You just didn't talk bad about Pappy and get any courtesy from Mom.

It took seven tries, but the bond issue finally passed and the school was built on what is now New Haven Rd., just east of Highway 63. Two or three additions were added on over the years, and when I was on the Board we got another bond issue passed and built Cedar Ridge school about 3 miles north of New Haven. Eventually the whole district got annexed into the Columbia school system. I don't really like it, but that's considered progress.

*   *   *   *   *

Orville Fowler rented a farm for 40 some years not too far from David Allen's place. When I remember him he was an older gentleman, and from what little I was around him he always seemed like an old grouch. John Paul Allen worked for Mr. Fowler quite a bit when he was growing up and he said the old man wasn't nearly as grumpy as he seemed, but I wasn't around him that much, so I'll always remember him as an old grouch.

One morning I was at Walkup's Station when Mr. Fowler came in with a flat tire in the back of his truck. It was off of his feeding tractor, and you couldn't hardly tell it was a wheel and tire for all of the mud and cow shit that was glommed all over it. He dumped it out on the parking lot and told Carver Walkup that he would pick it up later. Carver had a stock pond in the pasture south of the Station. He looked at that muddy, sloppy, shitty mess of a tire, then said "Mr. Fowler, toss that thing over the fence and roll it down to the pond, then wash it off. Wash it off really good, and when you get all of that mud and manure off, roll it back up here and I'll see if I can fix it for you."

The old man wasn't happy about it, but he got that tire wallered up over the fence and took it to the pond, and when he rolled it back up to the Station it actually looked like a wheel and tire. Carver jumped right on it, and before long Mr. Fowler was headed back down the road with a repaired tire in the back of his truck. Carver said, "He did that to me once before and got away with it, and I made up my mind it was never gonna happen again."

*   *   *   *   *

During one of the dry years back in the early 80s, Marlon Landhuis no tilled around 30 acres of beans into wheat stubble. In the swogs the beans got close to knee-high, on the thinner ground they were six-inches-to-a-foot-tall and on the real tough clay knobs they didn't even come up.

In early September Marlon called and wanted me to bale his beans for him. I went and checked them and it was a pretty sorry looking mess. There were some beans, with lots of rag weeds and badly weathered wheat stubble, but since poor hay beats no hay at all I agreed to do it for him. As Russell Coats once said "It'll beat a snowball."

When I started mowing I noticed the beans were in strips of 10 rows of beans, then 2 skip rows, then 10 more rows of beans and 2 skip rows, for as far into the field as I could see. I eventually came across one of the seed hoppers off of Marlon's planter, laying in the field between two rows. I mowed around the hopper and as I was leaving for home that evening I told Marlon where it was laying. He said, "I knew it was gone, but I didn't have any idea what happened to it." The hoppers held a bushel each, so that meant he had planted the last 6 acres in the field without ever looking behind him to see if everything was working. That was pretty much how Marlon did things at all times.

Fueled by Beer

It seems like there was always something going on in the neighborhood that would've worked a lot better, or maybe not happened at all, if it hadn't been for Bud Light, Stag and Red White and Blue. However, there was always enough of that stuff around to keep things moving right along.

*　　*　　*　　*　　*

Justin and Clint spent a lot of time with me when they were little. Whenever I'd open a beer, which ever one was with me got to suck the bubbles off the top before I took the first drink. One day when Justin was four or five years old I picked him up fairly early, and he was with me 'til almost dark. When I saw Kadi the next day she remarked that I must've really worn Justin out the day before, because he took a four-hour nap as soon as he got home. I thought "Ummm, maybe I ought to go a little lighter on the bubbles next time."

*　　*　　*　　*　　*

Not many years after the Bradleys' bought Tom and Velda Davison's house just west of us, they went to Colorado on vacation and Jeff brought some wheat beer with him when they came home. One Saturday afternoon I was out at the machine shed when Jeff drove up in his little Toyota pickup, with a cooler of wheat beer in the back for me to sample. He had three or four different varieties, and over a period of time we sampled them all twice, and then drank a couple more of our favorites. It was all pretty good, and it damn sure had a kick to it.

Along about this time the conversation made it around to trucks, and Jeff remarked that his little Toyota was probably tougher than my 3/4-ton Dodge. Looking back, it seems like there was probably someone else there kind of egging things on, but I don't remember who it was.

Anyhow, Jeff and I wound up in the road with our trucks hooked together with a good stout log chain. We eased up and took the slack out of the chain and then took off in a cloud of dust. Jeff's truck was so much lighter than mine that it was no contest. I drug him all the way to his driveway with his wheels spinning and gravel flying. I thought about going further, but as I picked up speed Jeff was starting to weave quite a bit, and I didn't think we needed our trucks wadded up together in the middle of the road. When I stopped Jeff got out of his truck and said I started before he was ready. I asked him if he wanted to try it again, but he decided we ought to just quit while the quitting was good.

*   *   *   *   *

It seems like 4 WD trucks and beer just kind of go together. I was over at James Earl's Parlor one afternoon, and his brother Russell was there, along with several other people. Russell had a 4 WD Dodge pickup, about the same age as mine. Every time Russell opened another beer his truck got a little tougher. Finally, we backed them up to each other in front of James Earl's machine shed. Before we got the chain hooked up James Earl came

running out of out of the
Parlor and hollered "If you
idiots want to tear your trucks
up get your dumb asses out in
the middle of Rangeline Road,
you're not going to dig ruts in
my driveway!"

Russell and I decided we
probably didn't need to get
out in the middle of the road
and draw attention to
ourselves, so we just opened
another can of beer and called
it a draw.

*Note: Russell passed away December 30, 2017, less
than a week after I wrote this story. Damn! The
good old boys are getting fewer all the time.*

*   *   *   *   *

Sometime in the mid-70s Joe Haley, owner of Bourn
Feed and Supply, acquired a six wheeled amphibious
vehicle. It functioned kind of like a clumsy 4-wheeler on
land, but it floated and the four back wheels turning
moved it through the water at a decent rate of speed.

One Saturday afternoon Joe and one of his buddies
showed up at James Earl's with the ATV/boat/deathtrap.
They jumped it out of their trailer and headed across the
barn lot towards the big pond. They drove it into the pond
and made it all the way across, then turned and started
back. The thing had a screw-in drain plug and it had been
just barely started. By the time they turned and headed
back vibration had caused it to come out completely.

James Earl, brother Russell and Linda Hickam were
standing by the lot fence watching this operation when

Linda suddenly said "James, I think they have a problem, they're getting shorter." James Earl said the machine was definitely setting lower in the water, and Joe and his buddy were bent over hunting for the plug. They finally gave up and started bailing water with their hats. James Earl and Russell threw out a rope, and with them pulling plus the wheels on the vehicle providing help, they managed to get it into shallow water before it could sink, but it was over half-full of water and just about ready to go under when they finally got it pulled to the bank. Joe never headed for the pond again without checking that drain plug!

*   *   *   *   *

One winter we had a lot more snow than what we usually do, and James Earl came up with an old car hood that he roped onto his 4-wheeler for sled rides. This worked fine until the beer took over, then it could get a little dangerous. One afternoon Russell and Joe Haley were at the Parlor when they decided to take David Grant hooding. Haley was driving the 4-wheeler, Russell was perched on the back and David was riding the hood. They whipped around in the snow for a spell, then Joe headed for the pond. He cut two or three doughnuts on the ice, then he pointed that thing toward the pond dam and cracked the throttle wide open. That little 4-wheeler shot up the dam and left the ground when it reached the top. About that time the hood hit the dam and it didn't go anywhere, it stopped dead! David rolled off into the snow and wasn't hurt, but when that hood stopped the 4-wheeler stopped in mid-air and slammed into the ground. Russell was tossed into a Multiflora Rose Bush and came out scratched and bloody but mostly okay, and Joe wound up with bruises in some rather unusual places when he slammed into the dash and steering wheel. It was a good thing that the car hood stopped them, if they'd have gone another 15 feet they would've slammed into a five-strand barbed wire fence. Sometimes Joe just didn't think these things through real good before he started. He never heard that old saying "Look before you leap." Joe just leaped, and then looked to see where in the hell he was going to land.

*   *   *   *   *

Before we added the room on the back of the house our family room was in the East end of the walkout basement, in what is now Stephen's and Kristin's room. The winter Justin was three years old we had lots of snow. He had waded through it up to our house one evening, and he was standing at the low toy table playing with his machinery. Marcia was sewing and I was reading. The outside light was on and suddenly Marcia said "Alan, there's a big chicken at the back door." I said "Huh?" and she repeated that there was a big chicken at the back door. About that time the chicken knocked, and when I let it in there was Joe Haley in a bright yellow full body chicken suit. James Earl was pulling him around the neighborhood on the car hood, and they were cold. Especially Joe: the chicken suit wasn't all that heavy, and why he was wearing it to go hooding in 20° weather I never did find out.

When I let that big chicken in Justin retreated across the room and stood next to Marcia. Justin knew Joe, but he didn't recognize him in a chicken suit with a beak and a big red comb on top of his head. Even after Joe took the head off Justin stayed with Marcia and wouldn't talk to Joe or even look at him.

James Earl and Joe stood by the wood stove 'til they eventually got warm, and then they headed out for some more hooding. The next morning our yard was full of doughnut tracks. As many trees as we've got it's a wonder that hood didn't get wrapped around a tree. It wasn't too long after that 'til the snow melted and it's probably a good thing, because someone was fixing to get screwed up pretty bad riding that hood.

*   *   *   *   *

Each year on the last night of the Boone County Fair, after the carnival was closed and all of the crowd had gone home, the Fair Board members and wives would head for the bumper cars at the carnival, then we'd have a ball for the next hour or so, riding for free and acting like a bunch of happy overgrown kids.

A couple of adults made a pretty good load for a bumper car, and when 2 or 3 cars would get someone pinned down, and continuously slam into them, or maybe 2 cars would hit head-on, we've been known to buckle a little sheet metal and occasionally Don Evans would say "Hey, you all are getting a little rough on my equipment," but when they invited us to ride they knew that was going to happen and Don or John never complained about it too much.

All in all, it was pretty much a fun way to wind up a week of work at the fair. I miss the way the old fair used to be, and I hope the Boone County Commissioners are really proud of what they've done!

Cars, Trucks, and Drivers

I saw in the paper recently where Dickie Bassnett had died. When I was a sophomore in Hickman High School Dickie and Elra Sapp were juniors. One night I had ridden with Elra to an FFA meeting at school. After the meeting Elra and I, Russell Wade, probably Billie Strawn, and maybe a couple of other boys were getting into Elra's Dad's '55 Ford, and Dickie and a couple of boys were getting into a '55 Chevy second edition pickup owned by Dickie's Dad, Carl.

As Dickie got in the truck he hollered at Elra "Race you to the Playboy Drive-in, by way of Woodlandville!" He headed across the parking lot with tires squalling, and turned west on the Business Loop, laying a strip of rubber that just wouldn't quit, with Elra right on his bumper. We

1957. Elra Sapp with Vencil's '55 Ford.

went west past Memorial Cemetery, north on Route E several miles to Wilhite Road, then west on gravel to Woodlandville. The dust was so thick we couldn't see anything. Russell lived in that area, and he was peering through the windshield and sometimes the side glass, watching for landmarks and telling Elra when to slow down for curves. We finally made it to Woodlandville in one piece, then headed south on Route J to Highway 40, east to the new I-70, then through town on the Business Loop to the Playboy Drive-in. Elra drove that Ford as hard as it's possible to drive a '55 Ford, but when we got

to the Playboy and walked in Dickie and the other boys had already been served and were sitting there drinking Cokes. That was undoubtedly the runningist stock pickup I ever saw in my life.

Looking back at all the fast cars and trucks we messed with, it's a wonder any of us made it 'til we were 21. Butch Purcell, who I grew up with, was one who didn't make it.

Me and Butch Purcell.

*   *   *   *   *

When I was 16 years old I thought I had to have a car. Pappy pretty much let me use his '51 Chevy whenever I wanted to, but I wanted a car of my own.

Carver Walkup's Son-in-law, Poodle McDow, puttered around buying and selling cars occasionally and he had a 1950 or '51 Mercury sitting at Walkup's Station. I really wanted a big old ugly Hudson, but I hadn't found one and I wanted a car right now, so I settled for the Mercury. It was big, heavy, sluggish, and any shocks that had once been on it had blown out long ago, but once I eventually got it up to speed it was a running son of a bitch. It was also a $325 money pit!

Before long the automatic transmission started slipping, so I took it to Leon McKee (Wanda's Dad) on Clark Lane, and he worked on it. He told me it would last for a while, but he said everything in it was pretty much worn out. It did last for a while, but it was a pretty short while.

Me, Marcia, Judy Pemberton, and Elra Sapp enjoying "Dog Patch" at Bagnell Dam. My old Mercury made it all the way to the lake. August, 1959.

Billy Butzin's Dad, Carl Timmons, had bought a farm east of Route Z, back towards Cedar Creek, and there was a '49 Mercury parked in the fence row. Carl told me I could have the old car, so me, Billy, and Elra Sapp drug it from Route Z down to Pappy's. The only problem was it had a standard transmission and I soon found out I would have to change the steering column to use it. I didn't have the tools or the workspace for a project like that, so I drug it and my other Mercury to Jack Fitch's Dad's place just south of Prathersville, and Jack and Mike Galbreath made the switch for me. I had to be really careful with the car after that because it was an overdrive transmission and it liked to shift out of overdrive on its own, but it would shift into neutral instead of standard drive. I'd coast to a stop, jerk the hell out of the gearshift, cuss a little and stomp on the clutch several times and eventually it would shift into something.

I was driving past John Riddick Volkswagen one afternoon when I spotted a red and white 1955 Chevy two-door hardtop sitting in his lot. I pulled in and traded that Mercury for the prettiest car that I ever owned in my life. I was still driving that Chevy when Marcia and I got married in 1961.

Me and Marcia with my '55 Chevy. September 1960.

Ready to go "Honeymooning" in the 1955 Chevy. June 25th, 1961.

*   *   *   *   *

Elra Sapp's younger brothers Larry and Jim used to piggyback with Elra and I. It didn't matter if he was driving his dad's '55 Ford or if we were in my old Mercury, we'd drop them off in town at a movie, then Elra and I would go do whatever. Sometimes whatever covered quite a bit of

Russel Sapp on his John Deere pedal tractor. My old Mercury is in the background. Late 1950s

territory, and a pretty wide variety of activities, and it wasn't unusual for Billie Strawn to be involved before the night was over.

Larry and Jim had to make their way across town from the movie to the Playboy Drive-in the best way they could, and if they were lucky we'd remember to pick them up before we went home. Russell wasn't old enough to go, he just stayed home and wished that he was.

*   *   *   *   *

I was watching a re-run of Hee-Haw a while back, and when Junior Samples kicked the front bumper of an Edsel and then went into his car salesman mode, it reminded me of when Edsels' first came out in the late 1950's. Andy Watson, Jim and Tom's older brother, bought one of the first one's sold around Columbia. I don't remember how long he had it, but it seemed like that ugly thing ran up and down our road for quite a spell. Edsels' were kind of like cockroaches; it was a lot easier to get them then it was to get rid of them.

Shortly after that someone in our neighborhood bought a green Edsel station wagon. It seems to me like it was Clarence Crawford, but if it wasn't him I apologize to his family for even suggesting such a thing. But I still think that's who it was. If possible, Edsel station wagons were even uglier than Edsel cars, and that made them pretty damn ugly!

*   *   *   *   *

Pappy never wasted a whole lot of money trading vehicles. When I can first remember he had a 1937 Chevy two-door sedan, and in the mid-'50s he traded for a 1951

Chevy two-door sedan. When Charlie Hall sold his farm to Rock Bridge Park in the early '60s, Pappy bought a 1952 or '53 Dodge pickup from Charlie and used it around the farm for a while, but it was never licensed. In 1967 Pappy told me he was going to trade the Dodge pickup and the '51 Chevy car for a new pickup. He gave me his little smile and said if I'd never driven that car it would still be good for a lot of years yet, and I 'spect he was right.

Pappy always kept his car in the garage north of the house. It was pretty small, having been built for buggies and Model T Fords. Pappy went to Allton Automobile Company and test drove a 1967 Ford short bed pickup. He brought it home and pulled into the garage, but the truck was about 6 inches too long and the doors wouldn't shut. Then he tried a '67 Chevy pickup. When he put the front bumper against the end of the garage the doors would swing shut, just touching the back bumper. That's how he made the decision to buy a Chevy. He was still driving that truck when he passed away in February 1982, and it had less than 40,000 miles on the odometer. Norm Beal bought the truck from Mom and drove it for several years after that.

*   *   *   *   *

Back in the early 1970's John Brown and I worked for Natkin and Company on the Moberly Prison, and we swapped rides. Actually, we swapped vehicles every other week, but I did all the driving. For some reason the State of Missouri had requested that John not drive for a couple of years, but he'd slip through the back roads to my house, and we'd leave from there.

For a week John would drive his 1969 Ford Thunderbird to my house, then I would drive it to the Prison and we would arrive in style. The next week he'd leave the Thunderbird in my driveway and we'd go to Moberly in my 1965 International pickup. That truck would have drug the City of Columbia if I'd had a stout enough chain to hook it up with, but maximum speed was just over 50 mph. At 50 it started to scream in protest and at anything over 50 the doors and hood tried to vibrate off the truck. Damn it was a long ways to Moberly at 50 mph, but we'd eventually get there.

*   *   *   *   *

Back before everyone started driving 4WD pickups, Gerald McBride bought a new 2 WD truck one fall. One morning that winter Gerald's hired man was driving while they were feeding cows. Gerald got out and opened a gate and the hired man started through. There were three sets of ruts that had been made when it was muddy, then they had frozen. The sun was out, and it had thawed just enough to be slick on top. The truck spun out, so the driver backed up and tried again with the same results. After one more try Gerald waved his helper out of the truck and got behind the wheel himself. He stomped down on the gas and headed toward the gate. The truck hit the ruts, bounced sideways and slammed the side of the bed into the gate post, just behind the cab. Gerald never let up and he drug the side of the bed on the post from one end to the other. He stopped, then the hired man shut the gate and got in on the passenger side. Gerald looked at him and said, "that's how you drive a truck through a gate when it's slick!"

*   *   *   *   *

Years ago, I was headed to town one morning with 400+ bushels of wheat on my orange Ford grain truck. By the time I got to the top of the junkyard hill the old truck had pulled down to less than 20 mph and cars were lined up behind me all the way back to El Chapparral subdivision. The mile or so from the top of the hill until I reached Old Highway 63 didn't have anywhere decent to pass, so all of the same cars were still behind me when I got to Old 63. When I pulled up to the stop light in the righthand lane a car pulled up next to me in the left-hand lane, and the driver rolled down his window and yelled "Get that damn slow piece of shit off the road, you stupid asshole!" I looked at him and laughed, then yelled back "If you're in a hurry you should've started sooner, then you'd be in front of me, you dumb son of a bitch!" About that time the light turned green, I turned right and he turned left and it's probably a good thing, because he was acting kind of pissed off. I actually thought it was kind of funny.

*   *   *   *   *

In September 2017 I was sitting with Richard Sorrels at the Boone County Heritage Festival at Nifong Park. Richard had his 1914 I. H. truck on display, and I had my 1950 Dodge pickup parked next to him. Every couple of hours Richard would pull the crank a couple of times, the old truck would start and we'd take a little ride around the grounds.

A group of people had congregated around the truck and someone asked Richard if they could hear it run. He pulled all of the necessary knobs, set the choke, then pulled the crank – and pulled the crank - and pulled the crank. He checked all of the switches again, then pulled on that crank until he got tired and then I pulled on it for a while. It never even tried to start. Over the next couple of hours we tried it several more times with the same results. I've seen Richard start that truck many times, and it always started on the second or third pull, but that afternoon nothing seemed to work.

We finally unhitched Richard's pickup from his trailer and I drove his pickup and pulled the old truck all over the park but it never fired. Richard's son was off work that afternoon so Richard picked him up, then went by his shop and got a winch. They returned to the park, hitched up, winched the truck onto the trailer and hauled it home. Richard told me a couple of days later that a shaft had broken in the magneto and there wasn't any spark. He took parts off of a spare one he had on hand and got everything back in good shape. Some of the things we do for fun turn into a hell of a lot of work occasionally.

*   *   *   *   *

An expanded version of this story first appeared in FARM COLLECTOR. Used with permission.

Me and the old truck; it was probably worth the trouble. September 2019.

On March 23rd, 2019, my Grandson Clint who recently returned from a 10-year Naval enlistment, went to Indianapolis, IN with me to look at a 1973 IH Model 1210 4x4 pickup with a 345 C.I. V8 engine and 4-speed transmission that I'd seen advertised in Hemmings Motor News. I had talked with the owner several times and he said the truck had less than 30,000 miles on it. I was a little skeptical about that, but after checking out the photos he had provided me with I thought the truck was definitely worth a look. Clint said that as long as I got him back in time for work Monday morning he would love to go on a little road trip, and I didn't foresee that being a problem so around 5:40 on a Saturday morning we headed east on I-70. The trip was uneventful, and with Clint coaching me from the GPS on his phone we actually arrived in downtown Indianapolis without missing a single turn.

After talking to the owner for a few minutes Clint and I drove the pickup 3 or 3 blocks, then locked in the hubs and checked out low and high range before driving back to the trailer. When we left Columbia I knew what the truck would cost me if I decided to buy it, so I took a cashier's check along just in case. I handed it to the owner and he went in the house to get the paperwork while we loaded the truck on my gooseneck. An hour or so after we arrived in Indianapolis everything had been taken care of and we pulled back on the road to head home.

I really love it when things work like this, but as author and antique tractor expert Roger Welsch would say, "hubris" was about to rear its ugly head. Some 50 minutes later and 20 miles out of Indianapolis, Clint and I both noticed a developing vibration, so I slowed down and headed up the next exit ramp we came to. Before we got to the top my 1993 Dodge dually 4x4 lost power to the wheels and we coasted to a stop. Clint laid down and looked under the truck as I checked all the gears and shifted the transfer case from high to low. He said everything was moving like it should, but about that time he noticed a hot smell. I shut the truck off, and by the time I walked around to the right side smoke was rolling off of the brake drum. The dual wheels had moved out 2 or 3 inches, and rear end oil was pouring out of the axle housing onto the hot brake drum. If something like this had to happen it couldn't have done it in a better location. 15 minutes sooner and we would have been in 6 lanes of Indianapolis traffic with no shoulder, and 5 minutes later we would have been beyond the overpass and setting alongside of the road. As it happened, directly across the overpass was a large metal building with several wreckers parked in front, and a sign "Curtis Towing and Truck Repair." I said, "Clint, lock those hubs, if the duals don't fall completely off we're going to see Mr. Curtis." The front wheels pulled us across the overpass, and we found an out of the way parking space on the lot. When we went inside they were sweeping up and getting ready to close for the day. I explained our predicament and was told that it would be several days before they could look at my old Dodge, but they said I could leave it where it was, and they would check it out as soon as possible.

I stood there for a few moments looking at clint and he stood there looking back at me as we pretty much shared the same thought. Before long I asked, "What do you think about it, young'un?" He replied, "We might as well, if we don't make it all the way at least we'll be closer than we are now." So, at 5:30 in the afternoon and 320 miles from home we unloaded that IH pickup that I'd driven less than a quarter of a mile, fueled it up, bought a gallon of antifreeze and a couple quarts of oil just in case, then we pulled back on I-70 and headed West. For the first 75 or 100 miles we heard noises and felt vibrations that weren't really there, but eventually we decided that this deal might actually work. Somewhere in Illinois we pulled into a truck stop and purchased new wiper blades because the ones on the truck were pretty ragged and we were driving towards some heavy rain, but other than that the only time we stopped was for gas and a bite of supper. As we were driving through St. Louis in a hard downpour, I remarked that this was probably the best thing that could have possible happened. When Clint asked why, I replied, "Because I never did like to pull a trailer in the damn rain!" When he quit laughing he said, "Paw-Paw, you're never going to change, are you?" The old truck handled really nice, and it also rode a lot better than I expected it would. We made it home with no problems and by now I'm pretty well convinced that 30,000 is probably the actual mileage.

After a year I've about decided that the old truck was probably worth all of the trouble it took to get it. I've driven it around 6000 miles so far and everything seems to be working like it's supposed to, so hopefully I won't have to do much to it for a while. Which is good, because a limited-slip rear end for my Dodge, along with an axle, hub and other related parts, plus the labor, wasn't really cheap and I probably don't need to be spending any more money on trucks for a while. Unless of course I happen to come across something that is really, really interesting.

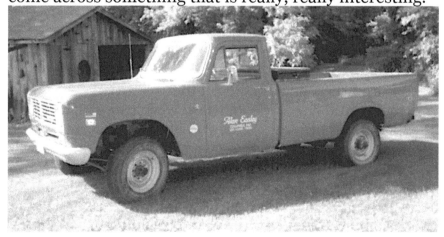

*   *   *   *   *

When I was a little kid Harry Seman used to come into Walkup's Station in an old Plymouth pickup. I understood Fords, Chevys, Internationals, Studebakers, and even Jeep pickups, but Plymouth's were supposed to be cars and I couldn't understand why someone would have a Plymouth pickup.

I also vaguely remember someone driving a Hudson pickup. I don't remember who it was, but Hudson pickups were so damn ugly that you remembered the truck even if you couldn't remember the driver.

*   *   *   *   *

One spring in the mid to late 1940s the Missouri River was coming up fast. It wasn't all over hell yet, but it was fixing to be. Pappy and Uncle Edward decided it might be a good time to try fishing in the backwater were Perche Creek joined the river. Uncle Edward had an old black, hump backed two-door sedan – maybe a Studebaker – so he and Pappy tied their cane poles onto the side of the car, dug some worms and we headed toward the river. Where the good blacktop roads are now there were rough, narrow and crooked gravel roads, so it took a while to make our way through Pierpont, Whoop-up and Easley, and then head north on the river road. That road was more mud than gravel, there were two or three sets of ruts four or 5 inches deep, and in several places where the road ran right at the river's edge the water was lapping onto the road. I'd never seen that much water in all my life! Uncle Edward didn't seem concerned, the old car was bouncing back and forth from one set of ruts to another, but he just kept on driving while he and Pappy visited. It wasn't bothering them any, but I was sitting in the back seat SCARED SHITLESS! I just knew he was going to drive into the water at any moment. I don't remember if we caught any fish or not, but I'll never forget how scared I was riding in that car right at the river's edge.

*   *   *   *   *

When I was renting the Murphy Farm, Jack Murphy had a 1957 Ford pickup that hadn't run for several years. Greg and Randy Blackwell were 12/14 years old at the time, and they bought the old truck from Jack for $50.00. We towed it home with a tractor and parked it out by the machine shed.

Those boys worked on the truck off and on for two weeks. They pulled the head and found one broken valve and one that was badly bent. They welded the broken one, beat the bent one pretty much straight with a hammer, and put it all back together, using high temp gasket cement and the old head gasket. They cleaned the carburetor, installed new points, poured some gas in the tank, then pulled that thing and somehow got it started.

Over the next week or ten days they fogged a lot of mosquitos with thick blue exhaust smoke and wore a hell of a track in the pasture as they ran the old truck in a big circle, as hard as it would go. One afternoon a loud bang and a big cloud of white smoke ended the driving, but the boys sure 'nuff had $50.00 worth of fun out of the old truck before it finally blew up.

*   *   *   *   *

When Greg was in high school he had a right decent green 1967 Ford Mustang, but it wasn't fast enough to suit him. I don't remember where he got it, but he came up with a really big assed, big block 400 C.I. Ford engine that had been bored out and had oversized everything, plus a racing cam. Just what that little Mustang needed.

Somehow Greg got that thing shoe-horned into the car
and hooked up to the little C4 Ford automatic
transmission that came in the car. He finally got
everything finished and took the car for a test drive. Our
road is gravel and at that time Rangeline Road was
gravel, so he drove halfway sensible 'til he reached WW.
On a straight line that intersection is about 1 1/2 miles
from our house. I was out in the yard when he pulled onto
WW and headed west. The engine bellered and the tires
squalled. When the transmission shifted there was a
slight break, then the tires squalled again. When the
transmission shifted the next time there was a slight
break, then the tires barely chirped before everything
became quiet.

It might've been Jeff or it might've been Randy
Blackwell with Greg on that test drive, but before very
long the two of them emerged from the woods back of our
house, they had walked across the fields from where the
car was sitting. Greg asked "Can we use your pickup to
tow my car home? It broke!"

He found another C4 transmission somewhere and
installed it behind that big engine. On the next text test
drive he made it about 150 yards further down WW
before the replacement transmission blew up. Before too
long that engine appeared next to our driveway, wrapped
in a tarp, and the original engine was back in the
Mustang. I'm actually glad those transmissions couldn't
handle all of that power, because that engine in a little,
light Mustang was a really bad-assed wreck just waiting
to happen.

*   *   *   *   *

Stephen in "Old Green," going solo for the first time. November 1998.

For years I drove a dark green 1977 Ford pickup with a light green salvage yard door on the driver's side. Jeff had his Mustang in our garage with the engine picked up on a hoist and he was backing my truck up to his car so he could load the engine. He was backing up at a fairly good clip with the driver's door open, but he had forgotten there was a pretty damn big Cedar tree by the driveway that was there long before we built our house. Splat! Sometimes those boys really made me wonder about them.

*   *   *   *   *

When Greg and Jamie lived on Robin Ridge Road down towards Whoop-up, Taylor had a small Toyota pickup that he drove everywhere he went. One afternoon he was driving on the gravel road that runs from Route 163 to Bonne Femme Church Road. Just east of Albert Gilbert's house, where the road makes a 90° turn, he was pushing the truck a little too hard and put two wheels up on the road bank, causing the truck to flip over on its side. I don't remember what his excuse was, but it couldn't have been any worse than the ones his dad and Uncle Jeff used to come up with when they were that age.

*   *   *   *   *

Originally published in Farm Collector, used with permission

In May 2015, I bought a 1950 Dodge pickup from Country Classic Cars in Staunton, Illinois. Someone had done a lot of work on the old truck, but it was still a long way from being a finished product. By some standards, it still is, but I'm probably not going to do a whole lot more to it right now. I'm just going to have some fun driving it around for a while.

The original flathead 6 engine runs good, the 3-speed transmission with column shift is functional and, after installing a new drag link, the steering is once again tight. The truck had been converted to power brakes, and the brakes had been rebuilt all the way around before I purchased it. The electrical system operates on 12 volts with a Chevy alternator, and I added aftermarket turn signals for safety reasons. I also had seatbelts, outside mirrors and an aftermarket windshield wiper assembly installed for added safety. The truck had previously been rewired, but the workmanship left a lot to be desired. After a really impressive spark shower one morning when I started the truck, that problem had to be dealt with.

Bruce Shull at G&J Auto Service in Columbia, Missouri, wore out a couple of good cell phones chasing down obsolete parts. Steve Bradshaw installed them, while Harry Blumberg offered lots of (sometimes) helpful advice from the adjoining bay. Bruce said the old truck got quite a bit of attention from other customers while it was sitting in his shop.

I liked the looks of the narrow whitewall tires that were on the truck when I bought it, but they were way too rotten to drive on. After I found out what it would cost to get a set of them shipped in from a specialty tire company, I decided I liked black walls better anyhow. Steve McCray at Cross-Midwest Tire Co., Columbia, furnished and installed the 7.00x15-inch 8-ply bias tires, two in highway tread and two in the old-style zigzag mud-and-snow tread that most pickup trucks used to run.

The truck didn't' have a back bumper, and I was hoping to find one from the late 1940s or early '50s that I could modify to fit. However, while visiting family members in Rushville, Missouri, my neighbor, Zane Dodge contacted his friend Mr. L.G. Rainey, who located a rear bumper from a 1950 Dodge pickup, complete with mounting brackets, for a lot less than I was expecting to pay for a "make-fit." After painting the bumper with a rattle can, it looks like it's been on the truck forever. Mr. Rainey also located a chrome headlight ring to replace the one that sailed off and landed in the middle of I-55 in front of a semi the day I hauled the truck home from Illinois.

Melloway Auto Body in Hallsville, Missouri, lettered "Dodge" on the tailgate and took care of some other little items that needed help. They also devised a permanent mount for the left wing-window that had a bad habit of blowing out and landing in my lap while I was driving.

From the 1940s through the '70s, Missouri law required that pickup trucks have the owner's name, town, and license information displayed on the side, just like the big trucks. I decided that since that would have been required when this truck was new, I would letter the doors and make it look period correct. The truck now sports 1950s-era door signs, only these are cut vinyl instead of being silk-screened like they were years ago.

The previous owner put a pretty decent "pass-by" paint job on the old truck. Sometime in the past it had been painted purple inside and out, but thankfully most of that got covered up with a rather attractive shade of off-orange. There was still enough purple showing in the cab to make me really appreciate the orange. The interior is now painted gunmetal gray, matching the seat and floor mats. It's definitely an improvement over the purple. The truck's not going to win any trophies, but it looks fine if you just pass by, and I don't have to worry if someone wants to lean against it or sit on the tailgate. If it picks up a scratch or two, that really isn't going to hurt it much, because after all, it's just for fun.

Kids on the Farm

It's a good thing that the Humane Society or some such organization didn't have anyone watching when Greg and Jeff were little, and then 20 years later when our grandkids were little, or I'd probably have spent most of my time in jail for child endangerment.

From the time those boys were big enough to walk they rode with me on tractors, in the combine and on top of hay trucks running back and forth on state highways. They wandered around through my cows, petting the gentle ones and feeding them ear corn, and I wasn't too concerned because they couldn't get close to the wild ones and the old pets weren't going to hurt them. Greg and Jeff rode and wrecked motorcycles from the time they were nine or ten years old and spent lots of time driving Ford Mustangs around on the gravel roads before they were old enough for a license. There's too much traffic for that now, but at the time we didn't worry much about it.

And just in case anyone is wondering, hell yes, they all made it! They grew up, got married, raised families and now there's a crop of great-grandkids coming on. I hope they get to grow up the same way the kids and grandkids did.

*   *   *   *   *

Randy Blackwell was the first one of the bunch to get a driver's license. One afternoon Jeff was driving Randy's

Ford Mustang north on Rangeline Road with Randy in the passenger seat. As he passed Tekotte's house Jeff saw a Sheriff's car turn south at the intersection so he stopped, he and Randy switched seats then Randy headed on north. Larry McCray was driving the Sheriff's car, and he stuck his arm out the window and motioned for Randy to stop. Randy rolled down his window and Larry asked "Randy, Jeff, how are you boys doing?" When they replied that they were fine he said, "Well I just wanted to check, I was afraid you might of hurt yourselves switching seats in the middle-of-the-road." Those boys never got much past Larry, but as long as they weren't hurting anything he didn't usually press the issue too hard.

*   *   *   *   *

When Greg and Kadi had the trailer back of my machine shed, Justin and Clint spent a lot of time at our house. We would turn the back lights on and they would walk across the yard after supper (or before) and when they headed home the porch lights would be on at the trailer.

Marcia was still working at the M.U. School of Journalism at the time, and one afternoon I had finished feeding and was home by myself reading or watching T.V. There was three or 4 inches of snow on the ground, and it was snowing so hard you couldn't see much of anything. Suddenly the doorbell rang, and when I opened the door Justin was standing there in his heavy coat, tee shirt and underpants. He was barefoot and his feet were cold! He wasn't much over four years old at the time, and that 4 inches of snow had come about halfway to his knees while he was walking. I got him inside and put a blanket and pillow on the floor in front of the woodstove, and got his feet propped up on the hearth.

After I got Justin taken care of I asked him what Clint was doing. He replied, "He's back there, somewhere.' That scared the hell out of me, I was thinking of all kinds of things that could happen to a two-year-old baby out in that snow. I made it clear to Justin that he was to stay in the living room 'til I got back, then I went on a baby hunt. The tracks were drifting shut, but I followed them around the house and about halfway to the trailer. Suddenly there were three sets of tracks, two heading toward our house and one set going back the other way. When I went in the trailer Clint was setting on the couch with his coat still on, and an afghan covering his feet. I told Clint that Justin thought he was following him to our house. He said, "Too cold, Paw-Paw, came back."

Katie was working nights at the time, and when she put the boys down for their nap she took one too, but the boys woke up first and decided to go visiting. I woke her up and told her that Clint was in the living room and Justin was at our house, then I waded back through the snow to check on him.

Clint doesn't remember that incident at all, and Justin was too young to remember all the details, but he remembers looking down while he was walking and seeing his bare feet in the snow, and how good that woodstove felt when he finally got to the house and came in.

*   *   *   *   *

When Justin and Clint weren't fighting, Justin was always ready to take up for his little brother. One afternoon when the boys were two or three years old we were in the machine shed when Clint did something he shouldn't have done. (Clint was always doing something he shouldn't have done.) I said, "Boy, you're not much punkins, are you?" He didn't say anything, but Justin looked at me with a really serious expression on his face and said, "Paw-Paw, he's some punkins."

*   *   *   *   *

Years ago, when the Boone County Fair was still held at the Worley Street location, I was on the Fair Board for several years. At that time the carnival was put on every year by Don Evans and Son Enterprises. Don and his son John ran the cleanest, most honest carnival that ever hit Columbia. If someone complained that they had been cheated at one of the chance booths or sideshows, it would be closed down immediately; Evans Enterprises wanted happy customers.

Back then the fair used very little hired labor, the Board Members did nearly everything that needed to be done, and we put in a lot of hours at the fair. Justin and Clint were around 4 or 5 years old at the time, and one afternoon after Marcia got off work she brought them to the Fair. When she got ready to leave, around 11:00 PM or so, Justin said he wasn't tired and he wanted to stay 'til I left. That was fine with us, so Justin held on to my Magic Finger and followed me around for the next hour or so. It was getting pretty late, most of the rides were already shut down, and Justin and I were making a last-minute wander through the Carnival as we headed towards my truck. John Evans had been selling tickets at the high slide that evening, and he was in the process of shutting down when we stopped to visit. While John and I were talking Justin kept looking at the slide, and before long John tossed him a gunny sack and told him to climb up and take a slide if he wanted to. He came down that thing laughing out loud the whole time, then he walked over and told John "Thank you, Mr. Evans, that was fun." John told him to go again if he wanted to. We probably visited for 30 minutes or more, and every time Justin came down John would wave him towards the stairs again. The last time after he came down, Justin said, "Thank you, Mr. Evans, but I don't think I can climb up that high again."

When we finally left John and headed for home, I 'spect that was about the tiredest, happiest little kid that I'd ever seen in my life.

*   *   *   *   *

One year a big yellow and black garden spider spun her web inside my machine shed. I was kind of curious how she intended to get any food with her web inside the building, but I shouldn't have been concerned. Justin and Clint were four or five years old at the time, and they spent the summer catching crickets, grasshoppers and any other bugs they could get their hands on and taking them to the spider. She got to the point that when she heard the shed door open she got ready, and when the boys would toss their offerings onto her web she would pounce, and in a matter of seconds have them well wrapped. She had enough meals wrapped up on that web to feed half the baby spiders in Boone County.

*   *   *   *   *

When Justin was little he loved my New Holland combine, and whenever I was combining he spent as much time with me as possible. One summer when he was around 2 1/2 years old he was with me at Bourn Feed one afternoon while I was dumping a truckload of wheat. He was wandering around barefoot, in a diaper with no shirt on. I'd finished unloading and gone inside to get my scale ticket, and I thought Justin was right behind me, but while Joe Haley was writing out the ticket I suddenly heard "Look Paw-Paw, flour." Joe kept a bag of powdered Malathion setting by the dump pit, and occasionally tossed a cup full on the wheat to keep weevil out of the bin. Justin had run both arms into the sack up to his elbows, then rubbed his hands on his face, hair and stomach. He was sweating and little rivers of milky chemical water were running down his stomach and soaking into the top of his diaper.

Justin, ready to go farming. May 1987

Haley and I said "Oh shit" at the same time and I grabbed Justin and we headed for the bathroom. I stripped off Justin's chemical-soaked diaper, then we rinsed him off as best we could, and washed the hell out of him with soap and paper towels, then gave him another good rinsing. I got a diaper out of the truck and fixed Justin up with a clean diaper, got him a can of soda, and then went back in the office to get my ticket. Joe said, "Oh God Alan, don't ever tell that boy's Momma about this or we'll be in a hell of a lot of trouble." I don't know if Kadi ever found out or not, but apparently she didn't, because I don't remember ever getting fussed at about it.

Note: Justin is 35 years old, and he has never been bothered by Weevil.

*   *   *   *   *

Jeff didn't just wreck motorcycles, he started with bicycles. He was still pretty small when Tom and Velda Davison built their house just west of us, and he rode his bike up there one evening to check the progress. The basement was dug, and he had up a little too much speed, and rode right over the edge. It didn't help his bike any, and he was kind of skint up, but it could've been a whole lot worse.

*   *   *   *   *

Back in the late 70s when everyone thought they should breed their cattle to be long, tall, wild, crazy and mean most of us were trying to get hold of a Simmental bull so we could accomplish all of those things at once. Good Simmental bulls were kind of scarce and pretty expensive, so when I got the chance to buy a three-quarter Simmental bull I jumped at the chance. He was about as calm as any other bull I ever owned but his calves reverted back; they were wild, crazy, mean son of a bitches.

Gene Brown's youngest son, Devin, was four years old at the most, and he didn't really know a Simmental bull from a Missouri mule, but he would tell anyone who would listen that "Alan's bull is three quarters Simmental and one quarter Angus." There was something about the way that rolled off his tongue; he just liked to say it, and he told everyone in the area what kind of bull I had.

*   *   *   *   *

Sometime in the mid-50s Pappy didn't have quite enough hay available to bale at home so he bought some "standing hay" from Dr. Nifong. It was in the field due west of Nifong Park, where all of the fancy student apartments are now.

Pappy mowed it and raked it, Paul Riggs baled it, and Kenny and John Cavcey and I hauled it with Pappy's 8N Ford tractor and a flatbed wagon. Driving back and forth got kind of boring and there was very little traffic on our road at that time, so on the way back to the field with the empty wagon I would run full throttle and weave from side to side to give Kenny and John a little more entertaining ride.

When I was a kid I don't remember that we ever used a factory hitch pin, we just used long bolts of about the right size, and dropped them in and let gravity hold them in place. That worked fine when Pappy was driving, but between swerving back and forth and hitting every pothole I possibly could, I bounced that hitch pin completely out of the drawbar. I happened to look back just as the wagon headed toward the road bank. John jumped and hit the ground running, and Kenny was thrown off into a reasonably soft patch of grass and weeds and just suffered a few scratches.

Pappy came down the road with the tractor and rake while we were rolling the wagon back onto the road. He stopped and watched for a moment, then used his favorite expression on me one more time; "Good gosh-a-mighty, Alan". I heard that expression a lot when I was a kid, but never when I'd done something that could be considered smart.

*   *   *   *   *

Kids definitely know how to keep us humble. My Great-granddaughter Lexi was about 3-1/2 years old the first time she saw me after I started growing a beard. She was standing in front of my chair with both hands in my beard, and she said, "Great Paw-Paw, you got whiskers on your chin, you got whiskers on your cheeks," and then with a big smile she said, "And you got whiskers in your nose!" Yeah hon, I sure 'nuff do!

Keeping Livestock

The last couple of years that Pappy had cattle his roan Shorthorn bull was getting quite a bit of age on him. Pappy knew that he ought to sell him but he liked the calves that the old bull got, and he also liked his attitude. The bull was calm and could be moved around without a bunch of snorting and pawing, and he wasn't a fence fighter. If he was in one pasture and the cows were in another one he didn't try to get there on his own. He knew Pappy would come for him eventually, and the cows would still be there when he got there.

When the bull was young and Pappy would turn him in with the cows he'd make the rounds twice a day, checking each cow to see if he could find one in heat. As he got older and heavier, and his feet started to bother him, he took the easy way out. Instead of following the cows he would find a nice shady spot not too far from water, with plenty of good grass, and he would take up residence. Two or three times a day he would stick his nose up in the air and

2015. My last batch of yearlings. When these were sold, I was out of the cattle business.

let out a couple of high-pitched bull bellers, to let the cows know where he was located. When one or more cows came in heat they would come to him, and I don't think we ever did have any late calves just because the old bull had gotten too lazy to go hunting.

*   *   *   *   *

One morning when I pulled in Mom's with a bale of hay the temperature was -10 degrees. As I drove through the pasture I noticed a new calf standing by the creek bank with its head hanging down. A cow that had obviously just calved was 100 yards or so away from the calf, standing at a hay bale eating. Apparently she had calved, then decided it was too cold for that kind of crap, and she had walked off and left her baby. The calf hadn't been cleaned off at all, and it was so cold that its eyelids were frosted shut. It had gotten up on its own, but with no momma around it had just stood there. It would've been dead in another 15 minutes. The calf's legs were too stiff to bend on their own, I had to force bend them so I could get the calf in the cab of my truck.

My female coonhound Leon was in the truck, and I wasn't real sure what she would think about a cold, wet calf in her truck. I opened the door and told her to move over and make room, then I stuffed the calf on to the seat next to her. She looked at me, then looked at the calf and started licking it. By the time I got to Momma's house the calf's eyes were open and the icicles were gone from its cheeks.

I left Leon and the calf in the truck, and then went in the house and asked Momma to get out some old towels and throw them on the bathroom floor, then I ran a tub full of hot water. When I went to get the calf Leon was still licking it, she'd kind of adopted it. I took the calf in the house and soaked it until the water heater couldn't keep up anymore, then I dried it off and laid it behind the wood stove. I drove out to the MU Dairy Farm at Midway and bought some frozen colostrum, and by the time I got back the calf was warm and ready to eat. I left him behind the stove most of the day, then took him home with Leon licking him the entire way and scattered two or three bales of hay in the corner of a stall.

When I went to check on him the next morning, all I could see was his nose and ears sticking out of the hay. His nose and lips peeled off two or three times from frostbite, and he lost about half of those ears and 6 inches off his tail, but otherwise he was okay. That was the coldest, nearest dead calf that I ever saved. He was one tough little S. O. B.

*   *   *   *   *

That wasn't the only cold calf that I ever saved. Years ago, when I rented Oscar Elley's farm on Rangeline Road there was 25 acres or so of rough ground on the northeast corner of the farm that was fenced off from the crop ground. I did some patching on the old fence and wintered cows there for several years.

One fall I had bought some bred "spec" cows at the sale barn, and they calved everywhere from late November 'til March. One morning in February when I got out of my truck at Oscar's little barn and headed toward the pond to chop ice I heard a cow bawling. She was pacing back-and-forth on the pond dam, stopping every few feet to bawl. It was evident that she had recently calved. When I walked up on the dam I could see a calf laying on the ice about 15 feet from the bank. The cow had calved on the pond dam and in its attempt to get up the calf had slid down the dam and onto the ice. The more it tried to get up the farther from the bank it got.

Eventually it had gotten so tired that it had given up, and it was just laying there on its side, holding its head up.

The weather hadn't been real cold, and as I cautiously stepped out on the ice it begin cracking after just a couple of steps. I retreated, and after looking things over I took a heavy oak door off the barn, drug it down to the pond, and shoved it out onto the frozen surface like an ice boat. I managed to slide it close enough to the calf that I could get hold of him, but I soon discovered that he was frozen down. His body heat had thawed the ice a little bit, but after he quit struggling it had refrozen. After twisting and pulling on him for a few minutes I managed to get everything loose except for the switch on his tail. I gave a big jerk but instead of the switch coming loose from the ice I pulled the tip off of his tail. He was so cold he didn't even notice. I got him to the bank and carried him to my truck with the cow following, trying to lick him as I walked. I opened the gate into the barn and the cow walked in, then I stuffed the calf into my pickup. It had been running the whole time and it was hot enough in the cab to roast a duck.

I threw some hay into the stall with the cow to give her something to chew on, plus enough to bed the calf down real good, then I started rubbing the calf down with hands full of hay. I always carried an extra flannel shirt with me, just in case, so after I got him dried off pretty good I wrapped him in the shirt and left him in the truck while I walked around checking the other cows.

By the time I got back he had warmed up, shook off the shirt, and was standing on the driver's side. His back feet were in the seat, both his front legs were stuck through the spokes of the steering wheel, he had crapped all over the back of the seat, his nose was pressed against the windshield and slobbers were running down on the dash. I was pretty damn glad that I didn't have a new truck!

I got him untangled, then carried him to the barn, lifted him over the gate and dropped him in a pile near the cow. She immediately started licking him and pretty soon he staggered to his feet and found a tit. By that afternoon he didn't know anything bad had happened to him.

When the weather warmed up that spring he lost about 2 inches off the tips of his ears and he never did grow another switch on his tail, but considering how he started out he was a pretty lucky calf.

Another rescue calf. Greg's dog To-Jo, me, Justin, and the calf in the old hay shed that Gary Chandler helped me build. March 1988.

*   *   *   *   *

I was thinking a while back about how much different hog farming is today than when I was a kid. Back then nearly every farm kept a few sows. There were a few small semi- confinement operations, but most hogs were raised on dirt. Pappy said if anyone had ever watched how much fun a bunch of shoats had rooting for acorns, or flopped down on their sides in a muddy "hog waller", they wouldn't have the heart to shut them up inside a building.

However, raising them outside, especially the way we did it, was definitely labor-intensive. The sows were fed in the barn lot, with ear corn carried to them in a bushel basket from an inside crib. The shoats were fed on the rocky hillside south of the barn, or in the rocky patch of woods on the west side of the road, that now belongs to Dr. Tony Spaedy. An old junk wagon full of ear corn would be parked on the hill, then twice a day someone would walk down the hill, climb into the wagon, and then throw out however many scoops of corn were needed for a feeding. Thinking about it makes it seem harder than it actually was; at the time that was just how it was done, and it really didn't seem like a big deal when we were doing it.

A sow at the old farm. Note the extra-tall fence; they were still farming with horses and mules at that time. Mid-1930s.

Hog shed and corn-crib on the old farm.

*   *   *   *   *

Pappy's cousin, Paul Cheavens, raised registered Hampshire hogs on his farm east of Whoop-up, and sold breeding stock. When he had a batch of boars or gilts ready to sell he would pen them together and price them for so much per head, buyers' choice. He told Pappy if he priced them individually no one would buy the lower priced ones, because they thought they were inferior quality. However, when they were all priced the same sometimes the lower quality hogs would sell first, and whoever bought them was happy because he had gotten to pick what he thought was the best hog in the pen.

I've bought bulls that way, and the breeder always said I'd picked a really good bull. I never did have a breeder tell me I'd just picked the sorriest S.O.B. in the whole bunch.

*   *   *   *   *

A couple of years ago Greg and Jamie left on vacation for about a week and I took care of their dogs, cats, chickens and horses while they were gone. They had an old rooster that was kind of mean, and the first couple of times I was there he ran at me and I kicked his ass pretty good both times. After the second time,

Greg and Jamie's new rooster is a lot nicer than that old S.O.B.

when I got home I went out to the machine shed and got an old ball bat that was leaning up in the corner and put it in my truck. The next day when that rooster came after me I timed my swing perfect; thowp! He squawked and squarked and flopped around, and it looked like I'd cut a feather pillow open in front of a fan. I was kind of proud of myself because I thought I'd killed that old son of a bitch, but about that time he staggered to his feet and left, about as fast as a crooked legged chicken can leave.

That was the last time I saw the old rooster, and when Greg and Jamie got home I told Greg what had happened and said that the rooster was probably dead. A couple of weeks later he told me "Well, he wasn't dead, he was just real sore, but when he started feeling a little better he tried me one morning. The next night we tried him and he wasn't too bad in a pot of noodles".

*   *   *   *   *

It would it take a pretty good stretch of the imagination to consider meat rabbits to be livestock, but this story had to go somewhere so I'm putting it here.

When Greg and Kadi had the trailer back of our house, Greg had several rabbit hutches hung on the outside wall of my machine shed. They had plenty of rabbits to eat, he sold quite a few, and the boys always had some baby rabbits to play with. One big old buck rabbit was kind of mean, and Greg started calling him Shit Head. Marcia didn't like that name, so her and everyone else called him S. H. Whenever my female coonhound, old Leon, and Greg's black dog To Jo walked near the cages they would raise their heads and sniff as they passed by. One day Greg was cleaning hutches when S. H. clawed the hell out of his arm. He grabbed the old rabbit and tossed it down in front of the dogs, fully expecting him to be eaten immediately. Instead, the rabbit hunkered down, the dogs looked at him, sniffed him real good, looked at each other and then up at the cage. They sniffed the rabbit again and apparently decided he belonged here, then they trotted off to do other important dog business.

You'd think that a cage raised rabbit would be pretty helpless on his own, but S. H. made it by himself for two years. He ate whatever wild rabbits eat, found places to drink, made rabbit nests outside in the summer and in my machine shed in the winter. If the dogs came across him they would sniff him and go on by. UNLESS he was on the wrong side of the yard fence. There was a five-strand barbed wired fence on three sides of the yard, and if S. H. strayed under the fence he became wild game. I've seen those dogs take after him more than once, and if they'd caught him before he reached the yard he'd have been dead, but once he got under the fence he was a yard rabbit again and the chase was over.

I came home from town one afternoon and something big and heavy had run over S. H. in the road in front of our house. He was about 2 feet long, 2 feet wide and 2 inches thick. That stretch of gravel road has been pretty hard on pets over the years.

Visiting Relatives
(Do I Have to Go?)

When I was a little kid it really didn't matter which relatives we were visiting, I thought sitting and listening to grown-ups talk was dull, dull, dull! I wanted to be home playing ball, fishing or just about anything besides listening to old people visit. I 'spect if I had listened a little bit I'd know a hell of a lot more than I do now, because I finally realized that old people are really, really smart. Some of us, anyhow.

*   *   *   *   *

It's funny how the world shrinks when you grow up. When I was still pretty small, three or four times a year Grandpap would decide it was time to visit "Cousin Jim" Anthony, so on a Sunday afternoon we would all crowd into the old '37 Chevy and head north. Way, way north I thought at the time. Pappy would take the old narrow crooked 2 lane Hwy. 63 to what is now Route PP, or Clark Lane. Back then it was just a rough, unnamed country road. Then he would drive for what seemed like miles and miles, until we reached "Cousin Jim's" farm. Then I would be totally bored for three or four hours 'til it was time to go home.

In the late 1960s I was employed by J. Lewis Crum Corporation, and Morrison Breedlove and I were working on the new General Telephone Company building on Route PP. One morning on my way to the job I noticed a white farmhouse setting well back from the road that seemed somewhat familiar. It was maybe 2 miles northeast of Highway 63, and it was actually in the Columbia city limits. On my way home I slowed down and took a good look, and the name on the mailbox was Anthony. It sure was a lot closer to the rest of the world than it was when I was a kid.

Three cousins: James P. Anthony, Doc Fortney, and Ed Easley Sr. The old shed in the background is the same one from the chapter Life on the Farm

*   *   *   *   *

As far as I know J.P. Anthony never did move away from home. J.P. took a little nip fairly regularly even though his mother didn't approve of his drinking. As long as I can remember there was always a non-running car parked behind his parents' house. He told Pappy it was his sitting car. He didn't drink in his mother's house, so when he would get home from work in bad weather he would sit in the old car for a while and take a few nips before he went inside. Whatever works for you, I reckon.

* * * * *

Dovie Fortney Lyon, who lived on Rock Quarry Road about where the camel and zebra farm is located now, was an old lady when I was a kid. Occasionally on a Sunday afternoon Grandpap would decide it was time to visit his old Aunt, Cousin or whatever kin it was she happened to be. Her house was old, dim and contained absolutely nothing for a kid to play with. It was at the top of my list of dull places we visited, and the only thing remotely interesting was Dovie's porch decorations. There was a long porch that ran from one end of the house to the other on the south side. She was a diabetic, and the porch was strung from one end to the other with little blue insulin bottles tied to cords and draped between the porch posts. They looked like strings of Christmas lights and tinkled when the wind blew. At least it gave me something to look at.

* * * * *

I was helping Jimmy Stewart doctor a colt one morning when he started talking about Dovie. The farm that Jimmy's dad owned joined Dovie's farm. Jimmy mentioned the blue bottles, so I wasn't the only kid intrigued by them. Jimmy said the day before he left for the Navy Dovie came walking across the sheep pasture in an ankle length dress and a sun bonnet, carrying an apple pie. She told Jimmy she brought it before he left because she wouldn't be around to bake him one when he got back. She was right, she died not long after that. Dovie was buried in the Fortney Cemetery in March 1957. She was the last person buried in the old Cemetery until my

Brother-in-law Jim DeMarce's ashes were buried in July 2012, and later Marcia was buried there in January 2013. I couldn't remember what month we buried Jim's ashes so I called Virginia, and started the conversation by telling her I was working on a story about Dovie, and Sis interrupted me with "And all of her little blue bottles?" Yep Sis, all of her little blue bottles.

The last three burials at The Fortney Cemetery. 55 years apart. Clockwise from top: Marcia Easley, 2012, Jim DeMarce, 2010, Dovie Lyon, 1957

*   *   *   *   *

Uncle Paul Cheavens was always one of my favorite relatives, but despite that fact when I was a kid visiting him and Aunt Susie was still pretty boring. No kids, no toys, just old people talking.

Uncle Paul's farm now belongs to his grandson Steve and Steve's wife Carolyn. Steve asked me one day if I remembered carving my initials and the date in the barn on his farm. I don't remember doing it, but apparently on December 25, 1956, I was pretty bored, either that or I had gotten a new pocketknife for Christmas, and I just couldn't wait to try it out.

Note: a couple of years ago Steve sawed that board out of his barn and replaced it with a new one. I now have the initial board on the wall of my machine shed.

Kids and Their Toys

Jeff's 1966 Mustang Convertible. Mid-1980s.

Jeff's 1979 Pontiac Firebird Formula, at the corner of WW and Rangeline Road. That thing was scary fast! Late 1980s.

Jeff and his Harley. Mid 1990s.

Jeff and Sam on the Harley. Mid 1990s.

Justin's first tractor show trophy. September 1997.

Justin pullin' the White Mule Sled. September 2000.

Justin. September 2004

Me. May 2005.

Clint. September 2002.

Clint. September 2004.

Clint. September 2006.

Stephen. August 2000.

Stephen. September 2004.

Greg's Minneapolis Moline "R". That thing would snort.

Greg. September 2004.

Clint with Justin's VAC Case. "What the hell do I do next?"
March 2001.

Greg salvaging parts. April 2004.

Me (above) and Greg (below) with a parts tractor. August 2008

Above: Bill Blackwell, Me, and Zane Dodge.
Below: Stephen and Zane Dodge with another parts tractor.
August 2009.

My latest toy. 960 Ford Tractor. Still needs a little work before I can play with it. 2021.

Leah and Daz at the Boone County Fair. 2008.
Masterful photography by yours truly.

My great-grandson Nico with his Rockin' Farmall. He was less than 24 hours old when I bought this for him. May 2021.

My great-granddaughter Lexi driving Jamie's Horny Lawn Tractor (above) and getting her Monster Truck stuck (below). Summer 2021.

Jeff, Justin, and Ford TW-5 pedal tractor. 1990.

Clint and my Ford lawnmower. 1990.

Some of the toys I've found when Zane Dodge and I were out roaming around.

Some more of the "collection". I know I've got enough but I'm still looking.

Some of the signs I've collected over the years (above).

Marcia's brother Bob found this one for me. (left)

This sign came from the old Henderson Implement Company and I bought the 8N Ford jack at Dysart Barnes' farm auction.

Damn Flats

When I was row crop farming it seemed like I always had a flat tire on something. I counted up one day and I had well over 100 tires, so it's no wonder at least one of them was usually flat. It's amazing some of the things that cause flats. Marcia's car was setting in the driveway one morning with a flat, so I put the spare on before I left for the field, but I didn't really pay much attention to the flat when I tossed it in the trunk. She dropped it off at Como Tire and when she went back to pick it up they said, "Oh yeah, that's the one you were driving in the kids sand box with." Apparently one of the boys had left a Tonka truck in the driveway, she had driven over it and an axle with one wheel still attached was poked in the tire when she dropped it off.

*   *   *   *   *

I was on my way home from MFA in Boonville one evening when a rear tire on my pickup went flat, fast. I put the spare on and drove back to Grotjan's Service Station and left the flat. When I stopped to get it the next morning they had mounted a new tire. Dennis Grotjan asked me "Can't you find a better place to store your tools than inside a tire?" Laying on his desk was a nice Craftsman three-quarter inch open/box end wrench they had found inside the flat tire. Apparently the front wheel had flipped it up and when the back wheel hit the wrench it punched through and wound up inside the tire. Dennis said, "I suppose you want to keep the wrench?" I said "I 'spect so, but I've got to find a cheaper way to get new tools, this isn't working out real well."

*   *   *   *   *

Nearly everyone who operates a tractor has run a deer antler through a tire at least once. Sometimes you just get a one prong puncture, but an antler can ruin a tire if you hit it right and poke enough prongs through at the same time.

I expect to deal with an antler occasionally, but last summer I was bush hogging the hayfield east of the Olivet Church parsonage when I stuck a deer vertebra in a front tire. That sharp little blade bone stuck in the tire about an inch deep. Luckily it went in one of the ribs on the tire, but even in the rib it didn't lack much going through.

*   *   *

Years ago, Turner Vemer was moving a tractor and disk from his house to the Roth place, and his wife Betty was going to pick him up. He got to the field and waited quite a spell, but Betty never arrived. That was before C.B.s or cell phones, so he eventually started walking back towards home. When he headed south on Rangeline Road he could see his pickup about a quarter of a mile ahead, sitting low on the right-hand side. Someone had lost a foot long piece of 3"x3" angle iron, Betty had hit it with both tires on the passenger side, and totally ruined both of them. Turner said "Easley, at least I got a real good piece of angle iron out of the deal."

*   *   *   *   *

Hugh Tincher told me that one muddy harvest season he went to Kansas and bought a pair of big, wide flotation tires for his combine. Flotation tires or not, he still got stuck and had to do a lot of digging before he was able to pull the combine out. After he finally got out he started to drive up his truck to unload, and he ran over the shovel he had used to dig out with and ruined one of his new tires. That wasn't one of Hugh's prouder moments.

*   *   *   *   *

Back in the '70s I was cutting beans on Brian Mitchell's farm in the field south of his house where the lake is now. As I turned at the end of the field and started back across I saw a tire laying in the bean stubble. I assumed it had fallen off a truck on the road, bounced over the fence and rolled across the field, but then I noticed some rather odd-looking tracks in the field. I stopped to check things out and realized it was a tire off the steering axle on the combine. My IH 303 had really good power steering, and when the tire went flat I couldn't feel it in the steering, and I drove 'til it came off the wheel. The tire was junk, but at least the ground was soft enough that it didn't hurt the wheel.

*   *   *   *   *

When I was working at the Deaf School in Fulton I was on my way home one evening in my '67 Ford pickup. I was sifting along about 85 mph when just east of Russell Coats' house I heard a clunking noise in the left rear of the truck, so I let off the gas and started slowing down a little. J.R. Jacobs had cut the beans in the field across from Russell's house, and suddenly I noticed a wheel and tire rolling across the bean stubble at a pretty good clip. I though "Where in the hell did that come from?" And about that time, I felt the truck getting lower on the left rear. I was probably down to 65 mph or so by then and it's a good thing I was, because when the brake drum hit the pavement sparks flew, and parts scattered everywhere. The truck came back, up, coasted a ways on three wheels and then went down again. It came up again and I made it almost to Olivet Church before it came back down. I steered hard into the gravel parking lot and got about 15 feet off the road before finally grinding to a halt. I walked back for a quarter of a mile, kicking some stray parts off the road to save someone from a flat tire, and then located my wheel next to the creek. The tire was okay, but all the bolt holes in the wheel were wallered out to twice normal size. It took a couple of trips to the salvage yard, but I finally found enough parts to put the truck back together. Bob Schultz came out one Saturday morning and we got everything working, and the truck wasn't any worse for the experience.

That isn't exactly a flat tire story, but it would've been a hell of a lot cheaper if it had been a flat tire. Actually, it did start out as a flat tire, I had a flat on my way to work that morning, and I was rushing to get it changed before some idiot on Route WW ran over me, and I didn't get the lug nuts tight. Shit happens.

*   *   *   *   *

Como Tire had some good employees over the years, Bruce Schull, David Vaught and Steve McCray come to mind real quick, but occasionally it seemed like they just drug someone in off the street, told him how to use a jack and a lug wrench, and sent him to the country on a service call.

One year in the early '80s I had finished cutting beans one afternoon in late December, and got my combine moved home before dark. I intended to clean it up and grease it before putting it in the shed for the winter, so I just pulled in off the road east of the house, where Stephen and Kristin have their orchard now.

When I went out the next morning there was a flat on one of the drive tires so I called Como. Before long some kid showed up who didn't hardly look old enough to have a driver's license. He damn sure wasn't old enough to know how to change a combine tire! He got a jack and a block of wood about a foot square and started to crawl under the combine. I told him the ground was kind of soft and he needed a bigger block. He went back to the truck and got a 12" x 12" about 2 foot long. What he really needed was half of a railroad tie, but the short block would've worked if he'd been prepared, but he wasn't. He got the tire popped off the rim on one side and pulled the tube out, but while getting the tire popped loose he had stuck one of the spoons through the tube. He said he would have to go back to town and get another tube. I said, "That's what I like, someone who comes prepared for anything." He gave me a dirty look, got in his service truck and left. An experienced service man would've blocked under the wheel and let the jack down enough that the wheel supported part of the weight, but he just left it on the jack and headed to town.

I went to the Ruggles place and put out some hay, and when I got back the combine was sitting there all slounch-wise with the corner of the header jammed hard into the ground and the tire wadded up under the wheel with the rim cutting into it. The kid said, "The jack sunk into the ground." I said, "No shit?" He asked, "What are we going to do now?" I replied "WE ain't going to do nothing. YOU are going to get your ass under that combine and dig a hole for a block so you can set another jack." He tried, but it just pushed the block down into the mud. By then it was getting dark, so I told him to call it a day and bring enough help with him the next morning to get this project finished.

It started raining around midnight and it rained 3 inches before it quit. The ground doesn't really dry up that time of year, and it was six weeks before it froze hard enough to support a jack. So much for storing my combine in a nice dry shed all winter. By the time I got done calmly and quietly expressing my opinion about this whole episode, Rusty Coats realized that I wasn't very happy!

*   *   *   *   *

Back in the mid-1970s Bandy Jacobs asked me to bush hog the south end of his farm. There were lots of small thorn sprouts in the field, and I knew I shouldn't do it, but I did anyhow. I spent parts of three days mowing, and when Marcia took me to get the tractor on the fourth morning, it was sitting at the edge of the field with both front tires and one rear one flat. Russell Coats at Como Tire made a hell of a lot more off that project than I did. DAMN THORNS!

Bits and Pieces

How long has it been since you walked into a restaurant and ordered a brain sandwich? Are they even available anymore?

*   *   *   *   *

I've always called the little purple wild violets that come up in the yard in the spring "rooster fights." When I was little kid Grandpap would pick one and hold it up, then say, "Cap, my rooster can whup your rooster." I'd pick one and we'd get the necks hooked together, then Grandpap would say "Pull." He nearly always popped the head off my rooster. It took me a long time to figure out that whoever pulls first has a lot better chance of winning. Grandpap could be kind of sneaky sometimes.

*   *   *   *   *

Did you ever look in your rearview mirror and see a Chevy pickup with both front parking lights working at the same time? Me neither!

*   *   *   *   *

I had a doctor's appointment in November 2017, and Susan Johnson told me she is retiring. DAMN! That's almost like a family member moving away. It seems like she's been my doctor forever, but we figured out that

Marcia and I started going to her in 2001, so it's only been 16 years. If my next doctor is half as good as Susan I should live for quite a spell yet.

*   *   *   *   *

I used to love to attend farm auctions, and I still do when I can find one, but it seems like most of the Auctioneers have gotten too damn lazy to stand up in front of a crowd and ask for bids. They seem to think that everything should be done on-line. To me an on-line auction is kind of like eating a jar of baby food when you're really hungry. It's just not very damn satisfying.

R.E. and Brent Voorheis calling a live auction.

*   *   *   *   *

In April 2018 I attended Virgil Gardner's farm sale up towards Woodlandville. Gene Sandner recently purchased Virgil's farm, and Virgil and Joy held an auction to sell everything they had acquired over the years. I saw people I hadn't seen for a long time, did a lot of visiting, ate a good country ham sandwich from the food booth and bought a couple of neat toy tractors. Just a hell of a good way to spend a Saturday.

Brent Voorheis called Virgil's sale, he's about the only Auctioneer left who has old-fashioned live auctions. I wish he'd have a lot more of them, every time I go to one of Brent's auctions he always tells the crowd that if they want to read a really good book about things that have happened in Boone County over the years they should check with me, because I've written two of them. I usually wind up selling two or three books before the auction is over. THANKS BRENT, I appreciate the plug!

*   *   *   *   *

Do you ever wonder why? I do sometimes.

*   *   *   *   *

In 2017 half of the politicians in Washington D.C. seemed to be getting sexual harassment charges filed against them. Doc Kincaid remarked "Damn, it's a good thing I'm a veterinarian and not a politician, or I'd be in a hell of a lot of trouble."

*   *   *   *   *

Someone asked me what I do since I sold my cattle. Well, I keep the yard mowed, brush-hog a little for some neighbors, cut some firewood in the fall, put out a round bale of hay for my Granddaughter's horses occasionally, and cook a little bit if I take a notion. In other words, most of the time I don't do anything, but it takes me pretty much all day not to do it.

*   *   *   *   *

Joan Sorrels, Richard's wife, said "Life doesn't last forever, but love does." That one sentence pretty much sums things up.

*   *   *   *   *

When Marcia died Betty Glenn told me "You'll never get over it, but you'll eventually get used to it." That's another sentence that pretty much sums things up.

*   *   *   *   *

The last chainsaw I bought lasted 30 years and it's still running, just not quite as good as it used to. In September 2017 I bought another saw from the new Henderson Implement Company in Columbia. If it lasts 30 years I'll be 105 years old. Someone remarked "Damn, don't you think you're being just a little bit optimistic?" Probably, but we'll see.

*   *   *   *   *

Thanks to old time country music star Johnny Lee for the line "When my life flashes before my eyes, it'll be worth watchin'."

You know when you're finally on your way out, if you can say that it's probably been a pretty damn good trip.

*   *   *   *   *

Momma had some really nice antiques, but she couldn't really be considered a collector. Once when a visitor asked where she got all of the beautiful antique furniture in the house Momma replied, "In this family we buy it new and age it ourselves."

* * * * *

If you see Clint, ask him how far you can drive on a gravel road with three garbage cans and a cardboard box full of trash on the tailgate of a pick-up; IT WASN'T PRETTY!

* * * * *

Did you ever fry stale biscuits in a cast iron skillet in about half an inch of bacon grease? Pretty good eating, and they're bound to be good for you.

* * * * *

It's been pretty hot and dry the past couple of weeks. I'm sitting in the family room on a Sunday morning, watching the rain out of the windows and listening to it patter on the trees. Kind of a pretty sound after a dry spell.

* * * * *

Aunt Mary (Pappy's sister) finally had to go to a nursing home at the age of 93. About a week after we got her moved in I stopped by to visit, and she immediately told me that she hated the place. I said that it seemed fairly nice, and she replied, "Oh, it's nice enough I guess, but there's nobody here except a bunch of old people, and I never could stand to be around old people."

* * * * *

When I was kid Grandma and Mom always cooked way more than they needed to for one meal. Biscuits, bacon, sausage, pancakes, pork chops, vegetables or pie, it didn't matter, there was always enough left to snack on all day, and still plenty for another meal. The leftovers were just as good as they had been originally.

When I wrote my first book I had some stuff left that I used in my second book. When it was complete there was still some stuff left. A few finished stories that there just wasn't room for, some nearly complete stories that needed to be smoothed out a little, some outlines, and lots of notes. I suppose reading this book is a lot like eating leftovers; I hope you enjoy these leftovers as much as I always enjoyed Grandma's leftovers.

*   *   *   *   *

Apparently the letter "R" is not considered part of the alphabet if you're raised in New York City.

Years ago, Momma was at a Easley-Cheavens Family Reunion one afternoon when she mentioned that she had given something to her sister "As a loner." Of course it came out sounding like "Asalonna." One of Pappy's distant cousins that she was talking to replied "Why Margaret, I didn't know that you had a sister named 'Asalonna.'"

*   *   *   *   *

A couple of years ago the Boone County historical Society Museum had a display of Boone County school items. I loaned them my FFA jacket, a couple of award plaques, and my FFA ring. The lady who was documenting the items looked at the ring and remarked that I must've worn it a lot for to show so much wear. I told her that I hadn't worn it hardly at all, it acquired that wear hanging on a chain around Marcia's neck for three years, before I finally bought her an engagement ring.

*   *   *   *   *

Don't tell me dogs can't count. Greg and Jamie's two dogs come over to the house three or four mornings a week, and I always give each of them three little dog treats. If I'm not out in the yard, or if I don't come to the door fast enough to suit them, they will stand on the front porch and whine 'til I come to see them. Sometimes I'll give them two treats a piece, and then stop, just to see their reaction. They'll stand patiently for a moment, then look kind of puzzled, then start bumping my legs and looking at me with a "What the hell is this crap?" expression on their faces. After I give them the third treat they wander happily off and do dog stuff, but never 'til they get that third treat. You better believe dogs can count!

*   *   *   *   *

Nowadays if you mention spanking a kid people look at you like you'd suggested starting a nuclear war, but spanking definitely served its purpose.

When our kids were little most parents still spanked their kids when necessary, but there was a nut fringe starting to form who disapproved of the practice. When the boys were four or five years old they were following Marcia around a sewing store one afternoon when Jeff looked at the display of yardsticks and suddenly said "Look mama, spanking boards." She said a couple of women looked at her like she was a mass murderer, but you've got to admit that yardsticks were pretty damn good spanking boards.

*   *   *   *   *

I was visiting with James Earl Grant a while back, and we were reminiscing about the old country banks that were in Columbia when we were young. We sort of ran through all the buy outs, name changes, mergers and acquisitions that have happened over the past 60 some years since we started banking, and we couldn't think of a damn one that resulted in an improvement. Sometimes progress is more like regress.

*   *   *   *   *

In my book "It Sure 'Nuff Happened: I Was There," I wrote about the advertising "church keys" that beer stores used to give away, and I commented that I wished I had kept one of them.

Recently the lunch bunch was eating at J.J.'s Café when Bev Blackwell handed me a sandwich bag with three church keys in it: one Pabst Blue Ribbon, one Schlitz and one Hamm's. She said after Randy read the book he handed her the bag full of church keys and asked her to give them to me. Thanks Randy.

*   *   *   *   *

"Big Norm" Anderson has been selling tractors and machinery around Columbia for longer than anyone can remember. Back when he started, if he wanted to sell a tractor he usually had to take a team of mules in on trade.

Last December I stopped by Sydenstricker's new satellite store on the Business Loop to look for some Christmas toys. After picking out a couple of tractors for Lennox and Rhett, my great-grandsons, I sat down and visited with Norm for a while. He wanted to take a closer look at my old Dodge, so we wandered out to the parking lot. Norm told me that he sure would like to go for a ride, and after checking his watch he said, "I'll make you a deal, give me a ride in that old truck and I'll get your lunch for you while we're out."

That sounded like a helluva good deal to me, so we climbed in and I pulled out onto the street. Norm said, "Stop at NAPA Auto Parts for a minute, if you would." As I turned in at NAPA I noticed that their parking lot was pretty full, and when we walked in the store there was a banner hanging over the sales counter that read "CUSTOMER APPRECIATION DAY! Free hamburgers and hot dogs in the back room."

Oh well, if I never get suckered any worse than that I'll be all right.

*   *   *   *   *

From time to time someone will ask me what my books are about, and I never really know what to tell them. I usually mumble "Just stuff. Kids, neighbors, Boone County history, just stuff." One afternoon I was visiting with Russell Coats when someone asked me what my books were about. Before I could answer Russell said "Life, they're about life!" He described them a hell of a lot better than I ever had. Thanks Russ.

*   *   *   *   *

When I was a little kid there weren't very many people around who were old enough to call Grandpap by his first name. Nearly everyone called him Mr. Easley, out of respect for his age.

By the time Marcia and I were raising a family most people called Pappy Mr. Easley, for the same reason. Now people are calling me Mr. Easley. Damn, it sure doesn't seem like I ought to be that old!

* * * * *

As I mentioned in my second book, when Marcia was proof-reading my first one she asked, "Alan, do you have to cuss so much?" I replied, "Babe, if I didn't they'd think someone else wrote it." When you read this one there shouldn't be much doubt in your mind who wrote it.

Construction Tales

Companies spend thousands of dollars on consultants trying to find ways to improve employee relations. Shorty Hathman, owner of J.E. Hathman Construction Company didn't need consultants. When the St. Louis Cardinals won the pennant in 1967, Shorty put a TV set on the first floor of the MU dormitory that was under construction at the corner of College and Rollins. The word was "Don't abuse the privilege and it will stay there." Workers would drift by and watch a couple of batters and then move on. Someone was always there but no one stayed long, and by word-of-mouth everyone was able to keep up with the score. It didn't cost Shorty a whole lot, but it sure made a lot of people happy.

Shorty Hathman was up in his 80s, but he was still sharp as a tack. One day he was standing by the counter at Columbia Welding when Jimmy Nichols walked up to him, slapped him on the shoulder and asked "Hey, Mr. Shorty, are you getting any?" Shorty replied "Why, are you missing some?"

*　　*　　*　　*　　*

It didn't really seem to matter much who I was working for, Crum, Jimmy Jacob, Natkin or some dinky-who contractor, most of the time it seemed like pretty much the same bunch of guys were around. Charlie Weyand, Jim Potter, Andy Rule, Tommy Dodson, Charlie

Lee and a few others always seem to hit the same jobs that
I hit.

Charlie Weyand and I worked together for Jacob
Plumbing on the West Ash Street pump station for over a
year. After we got laid off I helped plumb a couple of real
small jobs, then Business Agent Billy Harper sent me to
the VA Hospital. The first morning I was there Bob Victor
said that Charlie Weyand didn't have a working buddy,
and asked me if I wanted to work with Charlie. I said
"Charlie who? I never heard of the S.O.B." We buddied
up for about six months on that job until I got tired of
working for Wilkie and quit.

At that time Charlie was renting some slumlord
apartment northeast of the Armory. The State of
Missouri had requested that Charlie not operate a motor
vehicle for a while, so I hauled him back-and-forth to
work. Usually a couple of mornings a week Charlie would
still be in bed when I got there, but less than five minutes
after I kicked on the door he'd be in my truck, ready to
go. I'd stop at the Minute Inn and Rex Freemeyer would
fix Charlie a tenderloin and fried egg sandwich for
breakfast, then we'd head for the VA Hospital. Anytime
Charlie saw a well built young lady walking down the
street he'd stick his head out of the window and yell
"NICE LUNGS!" I'd say "God dammit Charlie, my name
is on the side of this truck." He'd laugh and reply "It's all
right, you're not redheaded, and besides they like me to
holler at them." Apparently some of them did, because
Charlie got a lot of big smiles in return.

*   *   *   *   *

When the VA Hospital was being built in Columbia,
Charlie Weyand, myself, Andy Rule, Jim Potter and some
others were on the sleeving crew. If we forgot to set a
sleeve or if one got knocked over during a concrete pour

it was a real hassle to get permission from the Veterans Administration in Washington DC before we could drill a hole through the concrete floor, so we spent a lot of time rechecking all of the sleeves and protecting them during the pours.

One morning three or four of us were watching a pour. As soon as there was concrete available someone dumped out Charlie Weyand's coffee and filled his thermos with concrete. If we had stopped for coffee at 10 o'clock like we usually did it would probably have been all right, but the pour was going pretty fast and we didn't stop until noon. As soon as Charlie picked up the thermos he knew there was a problem. Charlie was red headed and freckle faced and we could see the red creeping up his neck. He slowly unscrewed the cap and set it down, then he unscrewed the plug. The concrete was already set up, and Charlie looked in the thermos and then poked the concrete with his finger. He hollered "SON OF A BITCH!" Then threw the bottle off the sixth floor of the VA Hospital. If that bottle had hit a car it would've gone through the roof, and if it had hit a person it would've killed them, but we didn't hear any screams, so we eventually looked over the side and everything was fine on the ground. Everything wasn't fine on the sixth floor. Charlie was pissed, and it took a while before he got fine again.

*   *   *   *   *

When Jim Potter and Charlie Weyand were working together on the VA Hospital things had been running pretty smooth for a while, so they decided to stir the pot a little bit. They carried a 5 foot joint of 6 inch cast-iron soil pipe into the gravel parking lot, about 15 feet from the edge of the building. They dug a hole in the gravel about a foot deep, set the pipe on end in the hole, and tamped the gravel around it, making sure the pipe was absolutely plumb. Then they hung a 5 gallon bucket over the pipe, as if they were trying to keep anything from getting in and plugging the line.

It was a couple of days before anyone noticed it, but one afternoon Wilkie and Plumbing Inspector Lawson Nichols were walking across the parking lot when Nichols suddenly stopped and said "What in the hell is that 6 inch pipe doing sticking up in the parking lot?" Charlie and Jim were working on the second floor and they heard Nichols so they slipped over to the edge of the building, so they could watch what happened. If Wilkie or Lawson either one had pushed on the pipe it would've fallen over, but neither one touched it, they just walked around looking at the pipe from all angles while Wilkie chewed on his cigar.

They finally went to the shack and started checking blueprints. They were gone for half an hour or more, but eventually they came back and started looking at the pipe again. After studying it for a while Wilkie leaned against it. The pipe fell over and Wilkie almost went down with it. Nichols laughed, and Wilkie almost swallowed his cigar; he was pissed! He liked bull shit, but he wanted to be the one putting it out, he couldn't stand to be the butt of the prank, which made it that much better as far as I was concerned. Jim and Charlie had to move away from the edge of the building, they were laughing so hard they were afraid they would be heard.

*   *   *   *   *

I mentioned the VA Hospital sleeving crew in a previous story. Bill Wertman from Sedalia was our crew foreman. Bill was at least 20 years older than the rest of us, and he would just shake his head and smile at some of our shenanigans. Besides Bill, the crew consisted of me, Andy Rule, Charlie Weyland, Jim Potter and Bill Zumwalt.

A full crew had nine men and a foreman. I don't know if they thought the five of us could do as much work as most nine men crews or if they just didn't want to screw up four halfway normal guys by putting them with us. Andy was a little more laid-back than the rest of us, but he could stir up a lot of shit when he took the notion. Charlie, Jim and I were plotting something in the back of our minds at all times, and Zummy was a certified nut case, that's just about all you could say about him.

Regardless of all that we got a lot of work done on that job, and we had a hell of a lot of fun doing it!

*   *   *   *   *

One afternoon by around 3 o'clock, the VA Hospital sleeving crew, had finished all of our layout on the deck that was ready. We didn't really want to go down a couple of floors and run pipe for an hour and a half, so we were just fooling around on the deck, trying to be somewhat inconspicuous.

When we were laying out the decks all of the plumbers and pipefitters lines were laid out using red chalk. The electricians used blue chalk and the tin-knockers used yellow. That way, after the forms were stripped the different colors of chalk showed up on the concrete and it was easy to see who had what going where.

While we were messing around that afternoon someone suggested we should lay out some phantom sleeves and see how long it took the higher-ups to notice them. We found a likely spot near a wall and made three circles with our red chalk, then marked them 3 inch, 4 inch and 6 inch. After that we nailed down hanger inserts in front of the sleeve locations.

After the deck was poured and the forms wrecked out, those three missing sleeves shined like a diamond in a goat's ass. About the second day Bob Victor came strolling through the building. He looked up at just the right time and stopped dead in his tracks. He stood looking at those missing sleeves with a funny expression on his face, then he headed for the plan table. He spent close to two hours that afternoon looking at blueprints and staring up at that concrete deck. The next day Bob was back, bringing another foreman with him. They spent more time than Bob had spent the day before. If they'd have asked we'd have told them we were just screwing with them, but they didn't ask so we didn't offer. The next day those two were back with Wilkie in tow. He practically destroyed a cigar chewing on it as they checked prints and then stared up at the concrete. They must've been pretty sure it was a hoax but their pride wouldn't let them ask. Their pride and our bull shit cost Crum-Limbach about 12 hours of foreman's time over a three day period as they stood gawking at those three sleeves marked on that concrete deck. It couldn't have worked any better!

* * * * *

One morning when the highly talented, all business sleeving crew was laying out a deck, Bob Victor gave Andy Rule and Jim Potter the location for an additional sleeve. The only problem was he had taken his measurement from the wrong side of a column, and when Andy and Jim rechecked the location, by Bob's measurement the sleeve would've been 18 inches past the edge of the building.

They didn't let that stop them; they nailed the sleeve to a 2x4, slid it 18 iches past the edge and nailed the 2x4 to the deck. When Bob saw it he asked what the hell was going on, so Andy and Jim told him that was where his measurement said it went, and since they knew he was perfect and never made a mistake they didn't even question it, they just put the sleeve where Bob said it should go. That wasn't the only time the sleeving crew had Bob walking away mumbling to himself.

*   *   *   *   *

Back in the late 1960s or early 1970s Charlie Lee, his Uncle Alfred Lee, Kenny Fox and a big long tall slow-moving old boy from Kansas were working on the Fish Pesticide Lab on New Haven Road. Charlie said the guy from Kansas must have had a serious bowel problem, because he spent more time in the porta potty that anyone he ever saw in his life.

Natkin and Company had an old stub nose GMC truck with a Pitman crane mounted on it. There weren't any operating engineers on the job, so when they needed a lenth of cast iron water main laid in the ditch, Charlie ran the Pitman.

One afternoon the old boy from Kansas went into the potty for one of his extended rest periods. Charlie said there was a coil of heavy rope nearby, with a loop in each end. They slipped one end around the porta potty and attached the other end to the crane. Charlie lifted the potty off the ground and swung it gently back and forth a few times. He said the rope was high enough above center that there wasn't any danger of the potty turning over, but it was hanging at a pretty good angle. After playing with it for a moment Charlie raised it about 25 feet above the ground, then swung it around in a complete 360° circle, then reversed directions and swung it back around 360° the other way.

He finally sat it down and they removed the rope. The guy inside had said nothing the entire time. Charlie said the door eventually opened and the old boy stepped out.

His britches were pretty wet where pee-water had splashed on him while the potty was swinging around. Charlie, Alfred and Kenny were standing there laughing when the guy came out. He still didn't say a word, he just looked at them and then walked to his car and drove away. They never saw him again. He didn't even go by the office and pick up his last check, the Company had to mail it to him in Kansas.

*   *   *   *   *

J. Louis Crum could be an arrogant, egotistical piece of crap at times, or he could be just as common and likeable as anyone else, it just depended on his mood. Some of the guys that had worked for him for years didn't really worry about his mood, if they got a chance to dump something on him they did.

When the Howard Johnson motel at West Boulevard and the S.W. Access Road was built, each room had an individual heating /A.C. unit. After the motel opened it became obvious that the fan motors in the units had a rattle in them. The manufacturer furnished two little bushings with Allen head lock screws that were supposed to solve the problem. One Monday morning Morrison Breedlove and I were in the office at 5th and Broadway picking up 150 or so of those little bushings when Louie walked in. I was a 1st year apprentice, so I pretty much got ignored, but he looked at Morrison and said "I went out to the motel yesterday and put in a couple of those bushings, just to see what we were getting into. It's pretty tedious and there's not much room to work. It's kind of like jacking off a spider." Morrison never cracked a smile, he just looked up and said, "Well Louie, I'm sure you've had a lot more experience at that than I have, but don't worry, we'll get things taken care of." Louie said, "You damn smart-ass!" then he turned around and walked away.

*   *   *   *   *

Another time Louie walked in the office while Roger Moosman and I were picking up supplies for a A.C. maintenance run to Boonville. We talked for a little while about the three or four stops that we needed to make, then Louie asked Roger "Are you going to go 70?" (Meaning Interstate 70) Roger replied, "Louie, that piece of junk you furnish for me to drive won't go 70, we'll be real lucky if we go 55."

Once again Louie said, "You damn smart-ass," then turned around and walked away. After he had left the room Roger smiled and said, "We'll go 75, that way we'll have time to stop at Pete's Café for a cup of coffee."

*   *   *   *   *

I was working for J. Louis Crum when the addition was built on the First Baptist Church on Broadway. During construction the old boiler room underwent extensive renovation. The outside stairway into the basement was parallel with the basement wall, ending in a short landing with a vertical wall in front, and a door opening into the basement on the side. We were moving 21 foot joints of six-inch steel pipe into the basement by hand. We'd try to slide the pipe down the stairs without it getting away from us and hurting someone, then we would rope the upper end and stand the pipe up, then try to hunch the lower end through the door. Me, B.J. Dukes, Freddie Butler and Vic Jones were right in the middle of this process when J. Louis walked up to the top of the stairs and stood watching us. Dukes looked up and said "Goddamn Louie, this is a hard way to get pipe into a basement!" J. Louis looked at him and said "Hell Dukes, if it was easy I'd send you home and do it myself." It was kind of hard to argue with that kind of logic, so we just kept hunching 'til we got that heavy son-of-a-bitch through the door.

*   *   *   *   *

J. Louis Crum used that "If it was easy" remark quite often. Jim Potter was at the First Baptist Church, working by himself, installing an add-on drinking fountain. He had cut a hole in a plastered wall, and was reaching back into the hole, trying to tie into some existing pipe. He was hot, dusty, and bleeding in several places where the metal lath had gouged holes in his arms. Jim said he was using some extremely colorful language when J. Louis strolled up. Louie said "Jim, quit cussing in church! If it was easy I'd have sent some women and kids to do it."

*   *   *   *   *

I was working for J. Louis Crum when the dormitories on the southwest corner of College and Rollins were built. I probably spent more time on that job than any other job I worked on. I was there when we started running groundwork in the first basement, and I was still there when the students moved in.

They had moved in over the week-end and the kitchen was supposed to be in operation for Monday breakfast. At 2 AM Monday morning pretty much a full crew was there trying to get all of the equipment in working order. Wilkie, Billy Harper, B.J. Dukes, Jack Clemons, me and probably a couple of others were making final gas connections, then bleeding lines and lighting pilots. I never figured out how they got Old Pard (Jack Clemons) out at 2 AM on Monday morning to bleed gas lines, but he was there.

Since this was costing double-time, J. Louis was there watching the whole operation. I had been working for almost 5 years, but I was still an apprentice so Dukes was showing me how he thought gas lines should be bled. It was taking way too long to suit J. Louis, so he grabbed a couple of pipe wrenches, reached under the stovetop and loosened a union. He let it blow for what seemed like way to long and when he finally tightened that union there was a strong gas odor in the area. Louie reached under the stove with a cigarette lighter to light the pilot, and when the spark touched that gas it sounded like a bomb going off. The 4 ft. cast-iron stove lid lifted a foot into the air, before slamming back down with parts flying everywhere. It knocked J. Louis down, and he landed on his ass leaning against the wall, 10 feet from the stove. We ran over and helped him up, and he stood there kind of dazed, looking around. His eyebrows and eyelashes were pretty much singed off, and from his elbows down there wasn't a hair left on his arms. He rubbed his arms, then said "By God, Dukes, that's how you bleed the air out of a damn gas line!" Then he picked up his hat and went home. We managed to get all of the lines bled and the burners lit before breakfast time. It might've taken us a little longer, but we still had hair on our arms when we went home.

*   *   *   *   *

Eddie Moore, Hab McQuitty, Charlie Cartwright

Back in the late '60s I was working for J. Louis Crum on an addition to the General Telephone Company building on Cherry Street. Does anyone even remember General Telephone Company? Hab McQuitty was foreman, and he and I were the only two on the job for a while.

We had missed a sleeve in a 12-inch foundation wall, so one day after lunch Hab and I measured it out. The sleeve was for a 6-inch cast-iron pipe, so the hole needed to be fairly big. The elevation was at the top of the wall, so at least I could chip down instead of working into the wall surface. We didn't have a rotary hammer on the job, so I got a couple of big chisels, a 2-pound hammer, and a 5-gallon bucket to sit on, then I went to work correcting our screwup. The temperature was in the 90s, and I sat on that bucket and cooked my ass in the sun for three hours while I beat on that concrete. Finally Hab came by and asked how I was doing. I replied that I thought I was done. He looked at the hole that I had chipped out, then said, "Give me those damn tools." He sat down on the bucket, carefully placed the chisel, went tap, tap, tap with the hammer, and popped off a chip of concrete about the size of a pea. He looked at what he'd done, then said, "Now it will work. I don't know why I have to do everything myself."

Jimmy McQuitty, your dad could be a smartass sometimes!

*   *   *   *   *

At lunch time while everyone else was telling lies and tall tales, Freddie Butler would be reading the stock market reports in the Wall Street Journal. Someone was always commenting about "That dumb bastard sitting there reading the financial reports, like he was somebody important." It wasn't what most of us did at lunch time, but "That dumb bastard" didn't have to work at the trade nearly as long as everyone else, and he drove a Ford Thunderbird to work while the rest of us were driving raggedy assed old pickups, so apparently something was working for him.

*   *   *   *   *

When I was working construction there were always several good crane operators around Columbia. Fuzz Hazel, Doc Stull, Bob Schultz, Ray Hoffman, and several others, but the smoothest one I ever worked around was Richard Sorrels. I've set a lot of roof units with Richard, and if you needed a half-inch down that's what he gave you, with no bouncing or swaying. Setting heavy equipment is a dangerous job, but I always felt comfortable when Richard was on the crane, no matter how heavy the piece, or how tight a spot we were setting it in.

Richard Sorrels setting trusses at the Boone County Historical Society Museum, 1990. Most people don't realize how much Richard has done for the museum over the years. It's a shame he hasn't received more recognition.

*   *   *   *   *

Patrick McGath and I worked together on the Deaf School in Fulton one winter. We were working for Jacob Plumbing, and Patrick's Uncle Jerry was foreman. At that time Jerry was a Special Deputy with the Callaway County Sheriff's Department. This was during the Vietnam War, and one morning Jerry told us that there was a war protest march scheduled for downtown Fulton the next day, and the Sheriff was a little worried about what might happen. Patrick and I volunteered to go stand on the street corner with a couple of 18 inch pipe wrenches and help keep the peace if the Sheriff thought it would help.

Jerry laughed and said he would check, but he really couldn't see that happening. The next morning he told us that the Sheriff said "Tell those two crazy bastards that I don't want them anywhere near that protest march, the last thing I need is those idiots down there waving pipe wrenches." We told Jerry we were going anyhow, so we slipped off and went downtown, but the protest turned out to be a big fizzle. It was pretty cold that morning, and by the time those hippies had walked a couple of blocks with people hollering crude comments at them they decided they'd rather go somewhere and smoke some warm-up weed, so they never made it to our corner. But I still think it would've been interesting if we'd of been standing there in our hardhats and bib overalls, with pipe wrenches on our shoulders when they came walking past.

*   *   *   *   *

When I was running the Ramada Inn for Harry Bishop, I called the Hall one Friday and told Business Agent Billy Harper that I needed another plumber on Monday, if possible. Bill said he could send me Gene McGrath, but he couldn't guarantee how long he would stay. I'd never met Gene McGrath, but I'd always heard he wouldn't stay on a job for very long.

Monday morning Gene showed up well before worktime. I introduced myself and asked him if he'd mind running some copper. He said that that would be fine, so I scrounged up a set of tools for him and showed him what needed to be done. All day Monday, Tuesday, Wednesday and until noon on Thursday Gene did just what I needed him to do, he did it right and he did a lot of it. Noon Thursday he told me he'd forgotten his lunchbox that morning, and he was going somewhere to get a sandwich. That was the in the early 1970s and I haven't seen Gene since then.

*   *   *   *   *

When I was running that Ramada Inn job it was an addition/remodel combination, so the kitchen was in operation the whole time we were working. A couple of times a week I'd slip into the kitchen just before coffee time and borrow a handful of silverware and a couple of pies, then I'd take my contraband out where everyone was working and we'd eat Ramada Inn pie with our morning coffee. We didn't want to leave a lot of evidence laying around, so we'd toss the silverware and the glass pie plates into the dumpster.

The Baker for Ramada was a tall, long-haired hippie looking sort of a guy, and one morning he asked me if we could talk. He said "I want to ask you a favor, please don't steal any more of my pies." He said he baked a set number of pies each day, based on how many rooms were rented, and when we ate a couple of pies they actually ran out at lunchtime. He also baked some really good bread in individual sized loaves. He said he'd make me a deal, we could have all the hot bread we could eat and he'd furnish the butter and jelly to go with it, if we quit borrowing pies. I agreed to that, then he said "Just leave the bread pans and the knives by the door instead of throwing them in the dumpster, we'll pick them up and wash them." We kinda missed the pies, but we ate a hell of a lot of good bread over the next few months.

*   *   *   *   *

The old boy who was manager of the Ramada Inn at that time was from back east somewhere, and he just couldn't understand why a bunch of Missouri hillbillies who were working on his motel didn't show him a little more respect. We would have if he'd deserved it, but he damn sure didn't.

The day after Billy Butzin lost both of his legs in a hay baler accident I was going around the job taking up a collection to help Claudia with expenses. Everyone was handing me fives, tens, twenties, and I'd even gotten one fifty dollar bill. I finally walked into the manager's office and explained to him what I was doing. He asked if Billy had been working on the motel, and I told him no. He sat there for a moment then said "If he wasn't working here I didn't know him, but I'll make a donation anyhow." That tight son of a bitch reached into his pocket and pulled out two quarters and handed them to me. I really wanted to stomp those two quarters up his ass but I said "Joe thank you very much, Billy's wife will really appreciate your generosity!"

There's no telling how much those two quarters cost that tight bastard, because after that I screwed him every chance I got, and if I didn't get a chance I'd make my own chance. I really despised that sorry piece of shit!

*   *   *   *   *

Part of that Ramada Inn job consisted of almost doubling the size of the kitchen. The pipe was all run, the equipment was all set, and all that remained to be done was making all of the tie-ins so everything would function. The kitchen always shut down at 8 PM, and fired back up at 4 AM to get ready for breakfast, so we had an eight hour window to get everything done. The afternoon before we were going to do the tie-ins we went home at 4:30, ate supper and got a little rest, then showed back up at the motel just before 8 PM. That tight assed manager knew this was costing him double-time so he spent the night there watching us to make sure we weren't fooling around, but he was so stupid he really didn't know what we were doing most of the time anyhow.

By 2 AM he was starting to get pretty nervous about whether we would have things back online by 4 AM. He cornered me and demanded to know when we would be finished. I told him we had been working for six hours without a break, and everyone was tired, and so hungry we were getting weak. I told him if he would fix us a little snack it would probably help. He asked me what we wanted and I replied "That one grill and deep fryer are working. There are eight of us, so 16 of the biggest cheeseburgers you've got, a 5 gallon bucket full of fries, and all of the coffee, juice and milk that we can drink should just about do it." That cheap-ass had been thinking about toast and jelly, and I could see the dollar signs in his eyes when I said 16 cheeseburgers, but he wanted things finished so he fired up the grill.

We were 99% done when he cornered me, and by the time the food was ready we had finished up and pretty much had our tools put away. We sat down at a long table and ate, and I couldn't hardly keep from laughing while that sorry S.O.B. served our food and worked the table, refilling coffee cups and juice glasses. When we finished we scooted our chairs back, several of the guys lit cigarettes, and we sat there talking.

Pretty soon the manager asked if it wasn't about time we went back to work. I smiled at him and said that we had finished while he was cooking our food. We could see him doing a slow burn when he realized that he hadn't needed to give us anything, and we had conned him out of a full meal. He stood there and glared for a moment, then turned and headed for the door. When he was about halfway there I called out "Hey Joe!" When he turned around I said "Thank you for the wonderful meal, we really appreciate it." He just turned and stomped out the door, the sorry bastard didn't even say "You're welcome."

*   *   *   *   *

1980 was a hot, dry son of a bitch. By the time I finished combining wheat I realized that was about all that was going to come off the farm that year, so I came out of "retirement" and went to work for Bill Drummond on the Boone County Hospital addition. About a week later Bill brought me a 3-foot section of a corn stalk, marked in 1-inch increments with a magic marker. He said since it'd been so long since I'd used a 6-foot folding rule he thought I might be more comfortable measuring with something I was familiar with. I told him he was a damn smart ass!

*   *   *   *   *

I was drinking coffee with Andy Rule recently, when he asked me if I remembered wiring Dewey Phillips' doors shut. I remember wiring the doors among other things.

Dewey had a 1947 three-quarter ton Chevy pickup with a four-speed floor shift transmission. One afternoon 30 minutes or so before quitting tim I got a roll of tie wire from the ironworkers and went to work on the old truck. I wired the clutch and brake pedals to the steering wheel, the gearshift was wired to both door handles, then the handles were wired to the steering column and to each other. The truck had vent windows, and the steering wheel was also wired to the window post on both sides. I finally ran out of wire and had to quit and it's a good thing, because if I'd had more wire Dewey wouldn't have got it cut off in time to go home. The way it was he was a half hour behind the rest of us.

*   *   *   *   *

Harold Gholson was deathly afraid of mice. When the VA Hospital was under construction in Columbia Harold was working in one of the utility tunnels when he spotted a mouse. He rounded up all of the neighborhood cats he could get his hands on that night, and turned them loose in the tunnels the next morning. That solved the mouse problem, then all Harold had to worry about was fleas.

*   *   *   *   *

Harold and I worked together for a while when I was working for Harry Bishop. He lived in a trailer park north of Columbia for years. One day at lunch he was telling us about the good-looking 20-year-old girl who had moved into the trailer next to his. Harold said "She doesn't pull the curtains shut all the way when she undresses, and if I go in the bathroom and stand on the stool on my tiptoes I can't help but see her!"

*   *   *   *   *

In March 2018 I was attending Donny Gholson's visitation at Olivet Church when Jamie Johnson walked up and called me by name. I hadn't seen him for 35 years and he had to tell me who he was. We worked together for a while when he first started his apprenticeship back in the 1970s. He asked me if I remembered the first week he went to work, then he reminded me that we were running 6-inch cast-iron soil pipe with those damned obnoxious rubber gaskets. I was in the ditch and he was cutting a piece of pipe for me when I hollered, "Johnson, come here a minute, I need some technical assistance." He said he thought I must have a lot of faith in him, and he was feeling about halfway important as he walked over to me. When he got there I handed him a crowbar and said, "Help me shove this damn tee in that pipe, I can't get the son of a bitch to pop in by myself." Jamie said he still uses the phrase "Technical Assistance" whenever he asks someone to help him do something hard or heavy.

* * * * *

More often than not when I park my old Dodge pickup and get out someone will comment on it, and sometimes we'll have an extended conversation. Last summer I parked at Walmart one morning and immediately a new one-ton 3500 Ram diesel duelly whipped in next to me. The driver told me he had owned the truck less than a week and it only had 300 miles on it. He asked if he could take a picture of the two trucks sitting together.

We visited for several minutes, and as we were getting ready to leave he gave me his business ard. I looked at it and said, "Rick Parks; back in the '70s I worked with a pipefitter named Dick Parks, was he any kin to you?" He replied, "That was my dad." We talked for a little while, then I told him that before his dad built the machine shed on their place out of used metal roofing that Dick and I had spent three weekends at the M.U. Sinclair Research Farm salvaging tin off of buildings they were going to demolish. Rick said "Do you remember a little seven- or eight-year-old kid who ran around getting in your way all the time? That was me!" Damn it's a small world.

* * * * *

When I was plumbing it seemed more often than not I would be paired up with an apprentice. I don't know if someone actually thought I could teach those boys something, or if they just figured they'd start them with me, and that way they'd really appreaciate the next person they got to work with.

* * * * *

At least two motels and two University of Missouri high-rise dormitories, plus several carwashes, restaurants and service stations that I helped build back in the 1960s and 70s have been labeled obsolete and torn down. Damn, it almost makes me feel old knowing I've outlasted all of that concrete and steel.

* * * * *

For the past two or three years, one morning each month a group of retired members of Plumbers and Pipefitters from Local Union 317 get together at Hy Vee to drink coffee and tell a few lies. 45 or 50 years ago we used to get together at Chub's Club after a Union meeting or apprentice school. The lies were bigger then, and we talked a hell of a lot louder, but that was probably because we were drinking something besides coffee.

The Liar's Club is in session. Lloyd Calvin (Left) has everyone laughing. Clockwise from there: Chris Officer, Randy Poe, Daryl Bach, Charlie Lee, and Billy Gholson

Big John McCray. I don't know where he got his nickname

Daryl Bach

Left: Chris Officer and Jimmy McQuitty

Below: Charlie Lee, Billy Gholson, Lloyd Calvin, Daryl Bach

No Cougars in Boone County

Missouri used to be a wilderness. People worked their asses off for 200 years trying to turn it into civilized country, and they did a pretty good job of it. When our kids and grandkids were growing up, ages five or six and on up, they would go into the woods with the Blackwell boys, Chandler boys, Kevin Brown, Jim and John Lee, Billy and Gary Schultz and whoever else happened to be around. They might be gone for four or five hours but we never worried about them, we knew when they got hungry enough they'd be back.

Now there's an idiot fringe around who think we need to reintroduce mountain lions, wolves, black bears and God knows what else. I'd hate to think that my great grandkids couldn't go to the woods by themselves because of all the hungry predators.

*   *   *   *   *

For years people in Boone County have known that despite what the Missouri Department of Conservation kept telling us, there actually were a few mountain lions around. Maybe not a resident population, but definitely some transients from time to time.

Marcia and I saw one cross I-70 one evening just before dark, and when Marcia had that dumb, yappy-assed Abby dog, that thing pissed off something really snarly one morning just before daylight. I was leash walking Abby on the road east of the house when she went crazy barking down by the creek. She finally drew a response and when she heard it she shut up completely and got between my feet and just sat there shaking. I said, "Good dog, it's about time you shut up, now let's get the hell out of here."

I usually carried a flashlight, in case a car came along while we were walking, but for some reason I didn't have one that morning. I would've loved to shine a light into that brush patch, just to see what I could see. It could've been a bobcat, I'm not going to say it wasn't, but it was the biggest sounding damn bobcat I ever heard!

When Clint was 12 or 13 years old, one morning before daylight he climbed into his tree stand on the west side of the road at the old place on Bearfield. He hadn't been there very long 'til he heard a squall from about 50 yards away that scared the hell out of him. He said he was afraid to stay in the tree, but he damn sure didn't want to be on the ground. As soon as it got light enough to see he climbed down and went to Grandma's house. I don't think he ever went back to that tree stand again before daylight. Bobcat? Maybe, you tell me.

*   *   *   *   *

Luke Youngman has a freeze proof cattle waterer in his center pasture that sets quite a ways off the road. In the summer of 2016 I glanced in that direction one day as I drove past and saw a large cat with a really long tail. I thought "Surely not." I didn't mention it to anyone, but over the next few weeks my grandson Stephen, and several other people, asked me if I'd seen the mountain lion at Luke's place, so it wasn't my imagination. I hope that S.O.B. went off somewhere and died, we don't need those damn things in Boone County!

Guns and Fishing Poles

Back in the '80s I was rebuilding a stretch of fence on the old place on Bearfield Road. The weather was kind of cool and I was wearing a tan Carhartt jacket. What I had overlooked was the fact that it was opening day of deer season. I was working away just as happy as if I'd had good sense, when I suddenly heard a rifle shot from pretty close proximity. Immediately afterwards there were two more quick shots. I thought "Well, some dumb-ass missed, and now they're trying to hit him on the run." Then I looked down and saw that tan coat and realized that I was working right at the edge of the woods; I said, "Screw this fence!" I took the coat off and tossed it in the truck, then I started loading tools. I got the hell out of there and didn't finish working on that little dab of fence 'til after deer season was over.

*   *   *   *   *

I used to deer hunt, and I always enjoyed it, but if you kill one you have to drag it out of the brush, dress that stinking S.O.B., then either work it up yourself or pay a processing plant as much as the meat is worth to do it for you. No more than I eat anymore I'd just as soon go to the store and buy a few good cuts of beef. But sometimes I get to help drag them out, even if I didn't shoot them.

Me, Jamie, and her 9-point buck. November 2017.

Opening morning of deer season, 2017, my daughter-in-law Jamie climbed into her tree stand back of the hay shed, checked her binoculars, put hand warmers in her gloves, then picked up her rifle and shot a 235-pound nine point buck who had just stood up from his overnight bed. He ran about 200 feet, then jumped into the creek and died. My little Massey Ferguson loader tractor came in real handy on that retrieval.

A week later my grandson Stephen shot a nine-point buck in the orchard east of the house. It ran about 100 yards through the brush and briars, jumped a fence, and ran into the creek and died. We used the little tractor again.

Years ago, the first deer my grandson Justin shot ran at least 100 yards, then blundered 20 some feet out into a pond before it died. I'm beginning to wonder where a damn deer goes to die if there's no water around.

Stephen, and his 9-point buck. November 2017.

Justin's first deer.
November 2000.

Stephen and deer. 1995.

*   *   *   *   *

In the fall of 2017 a young lady in northern Boone County shot an elk by mistake, she thought it was a really big deer. If you can't tell the difference between an elk and a deer you probably don't need to be out in the woods with a gun, but I'm glad she killed that S.O.B., we don't need elk in Boone County. Deer can do a hell of a lot of crop damage; I can't imagine how much a herd of elk would eat. And hitting a deer does enough damage to a vehicle, an elk would be like hitting a cow. Thanks for containing your released elk on the Peck Ranch, Missouri Department of Conservation!

*   *   *   *   *

One afternoon years ago I was disking on the Schwabe place and old Leon, my female coonhound, was following along behind catching mice. There was a big Sycamore tree in the lower end of the field and as I went past the tree a really small fawn deer ran out of the weeds by the tree. Within 10 feet Leon had it by the throat. I got off and looked at it and decided that it was too much for Leon, so I took it home and dressed it, then put it in the sink to soak. It was so small it fit perfectly in one compartment of the sink.

When Marcia got home from work I boned it out and sliced it into frying meat. She cooked a couple of big skillets full, and when we started eating the meat it was absolutely tasteless. The fawn was so young it hadn't developed any flavor at all. It tasted like the flour and grease it was cooked in. I dressed it and sliced it, Marcia fried it, and Leon got to eat it after all.

*   *   *   *   *

When we bought the farm and built our house in 1963 rabbits were so thick they were a nuisance. Occasionally when I'd get home from work Marcia would say "Why don't you shoot a couple of rabbits for supper?", so I'd walk out in the garden and shoot a couple of rabbits and be back at the house five minutes later.

One Saturday afternoon Buddy Shaw, Herbie (Red) Ward and Wes Fewell stopped at the house and asked if they could go rabbit hunting. I agreed and said I'd go with them if they didn't care. We walked west along the fence row to Russell Coats' line, where Bradley's house is now, turned south and worked our way around the pond and along the fence row where Greg and Jamie's house is now, then following the creek we worked our way home. Less than an hour after we started we were back at the house with 39 rabbits. At times we were all four shooting at the same time, each one of us at a different rabbit.

Now it's kind of unusual to see two rabbits in the same day, and a lot of days go by when I don't see any. There's still quite a bit of cover around, but we're definitely at the bottom of the cycle right now. Rabbits don't hurt anything; I hope they come back thick.

*   *   *   *   *

Greg and squirrels. We always had fresh meat when Greg and Jeff were growing up. October 1975.

I used to spend a lot of time squirrel hunting. I would wander the woods on the homeplace, on Nifong's farm, and on Charlie Hall's farm that is now part of Rock Bridge State Park, for hours at a time. Squirrels are so thick now that I could set in my front yard for 30 minutes and shoot a nice mess of them, but I've gotten to the point that I'd rather watch squirrels than shoot them.

*   *   *   *   *

When Justin was eight or ten years old he was spending a weekend at our house. He wanted to go fishing so we decided to set out some bank lines in the pond. We knew there were some pretty nice channel cats in there because we'd throw out cat food for them occasionally and watch them eat. Cat food was cheaper than fish food and it floated just as good.

We had counted as many as a dozen nice big ones at the surface at the same time, and I'm sure there were lots more than that in the pond. The biggest one had a hump in his back like a buffalo. I don't know how long he was, but he was a damn big channel cat. Another one had been bitten by a turtle sometime in the past, and his lips and lower jaw were missing on one side. He would come up to the floating food and roll over on one side, then collect the chunks on his good side and swallow. It didn't seem like it really bothered him too much.

We baited three or four lines with squished together liverwurst and shredded cheddar cheese, jammed the cane poles into the bank as far as we could, then went back to the house and ate a sandwich.

When we got back to the pond we had fish on two of the lines. There was a fence across the pond, and I told Justin we'd better get the one closest to the fence first, before he managed to get through the woven wire and it became impossible to get him back through it. It wasn't any problem to land him, and he was a really nice fish, way too big to fry whole. By the time we got him in a 5-gallon bucket of water the other line was going crazy, jerking and bobbing up and down. I pulled the pole out of the bank and told Justin to pull him in, but he couldn't budge him. I took the pole and didn't have any better luck than Justin had. I was using heavy trot line cord and I wasn't worried about breaking it, so I planted my feet and then told Justin to get on the pole and help me pull. It was like trying to drag a dead cow out of that pond!

Finally, something gave way, the end of the pole sprung up, Justin and I fell back on our butts and the line with something on it flew back over our heads. When we retrieved it we had a really big catfish head. Apparently after the fish got hooked a turtle had started chewing on it, and eventually chewed it off right behind the head. I said, "Awe shucks" and maybe a few other things, then we got our one good fish and headed for the house. Marcia fried catfish steaks for supper and we had all that the three of us could eat, but I was still pretty pissed off at that damn turtle.

*   *   *   *   *

When Greg and Jeff were little that pond didn't have any catfish in it, but bluegills were so thick they couldn't hardly swim. You'd catch 15 or 20 2" and 3" fish for every good one, and it was a perfect spot for kids to fish because they could catch something on almost every cast. If you ran out of bait you could throw a bare hook in and something would usually grab it. The boys measured keepers on their fingers and their fingers were still pretty short, but we nearly always had some fish to eat.

We had an 8 hp Ford riding mower with a two wheeled garden cart back then, and the boys started out early each year and kept a path mowed to the pond. They would load poles and bait into the cart, and after they got the mower started Jeff would climb into the cart and hold the poles while Greg drove the mower to the pond. The boys were so small that neither one of them could pull the starter rope by themselves, so they both grabbed hold and pulled together until they got it started. Those two haven't worked that good together since then.

*   *   *   *   *

The pond on our place wasn't the only one with turtle problems. One afternoon when I was little kid Pappy and I had walked through the woods with our cane poles to Nifong's pond. At that time there was an old ragged assed, rotted out dock on the south side of the pond. It was so decrepit Pappy wouldn't let me out on it, so I was fishing from the bank and he was out on what was left of the dock. Fish were biting pretty slow, but we had caught a few halfway decent Creek Perch.

Eventually Pappy decided we might do better fishing off the dam, so he left the stringer of fish hooked to the dock and we moved around to the dam. After about an hour of slow bites and no bites, Pappy said we might as well go home and try again some other time, so we walked

around to the dock to get the stringer. Pappy didn't cuss
very often, but when he pulled that stringer out of the
water he said "Damnation, Alan!" A turtle had found the
stringer, and all that was left was a line of fish heads, the
good parts were completely gone. Pappy took the heads
off the stringer and tossed them in the pond, then he said
damnation again and we headed for home.

*   *   *   *   *

When the boys had C. J. and Bruno, the beagles that
they got from Tekotte, J. R. Jacobs came by the house one
cold Sunday afternoon and wanted to borrow the dogs
and take them rabbit hunting. I called them and they
jumped up in the seat of J. R.'s pickup, ready to go.

J. R. drove about half a mile west and pulled in on the
north side of Russell Coats' place, about where Luke
Youngman's house is now. He drove back in the field a
ways until he came to a fairly weedy area, then he
stopped, got his gun and let the dogs out of the truck. He
said they looked at him like "What's this all about?" and
then headed northeast on a straight line towards our
house. He never saw them again; less than half an hour
after he picked them up they were back home, curled up
in the sun asleep. J. R. told anyone who would listen that
they should borrow my beagles. He'd say "Them's the
huntingest damn dogs I ever saw in my life!"

*   *   *   *   *

Greg and I got our double-barrel shotguns one
afternoon when those pups were still pretty small, and
headed for a weed field to see if they'd track rabbits. We
worked the fence row between my place and Russel
Coats' place, went around the pond, and had made it to
the Southwest corner of my place without seeing any

rabbits. As we moved into the edge of the woods a squirrel ran in front of us, with the beagles right behind it. They chased it up a Black Oak tree, then went crazy barking and jumping at the tree trunk. After looking closely, we realized there were six squirrels up that tree.

BOOM, BOOM, BOOM, BOOM! We re-loaded, then BOOM, BOOM! When the last squirrel hit the ground I looked to see what the pups thought about the dead squirrels. I guaran-damn-tee they weren't thinking anything about squirrels, they were thinking about home and they never looked back 'til they got there. All I could see was beagle butts as they headed across the field as fast as they could run. After that those dogs always liked to chase rabbits and tree squirrels, and they didn't mind if I went along, but if I brought a gun with me they were gone.

I guess I should have told J.R. that my dogs were gun-shy, but it just seemed like more fun not to. I was that way sometimes.

Note: Always start pups around a .22 rifle, don't be a dumb-ass like I was. If a .22 doesn't bother them you can always get louder.

Only in Boone County

Columbia, MO., apparently has a larger percentage of thin-skinned people than anywhere else in the United States.

The Confederate rock which sat at the south end of 9th Street for years, is dedicated to Confederate Soldiers from Boone County who were killed in the Civil War. It offended the wrong people and it is now located at the Civil War Battlefield Memorial south of Centralia, MO. They were glad to accept it.

The Confederate Rock at the Centralia Battlefield site. The brass plaque reads: "To honor the valor and patriotism of Confederate soldiers of Boone County."

In late 2017 there was a big push to change the name of Lee Elementary School, and I'm sure it will succeed. I assume the name offends the same people who didn't like the rock. Thin skin and stupidity apparently go pretty good together.

A few years ago, a monument was erected on the Court House grounds to commemorate some young men who were killed in the Gulf War. Near the bottom of the monument was an etching of a "Jesus Fish." Some atheist prick threw a shit fit, and our wimpy assed County

Commission ordered the monument moved. It is now located at the privately owned Columbia Cemetery, and until it could be moved the commission had the fish on the monument covered. I suppose they were afraid of losing the atheist vote.

These are the same three assholes who caused the Boone County Fairgrounds to be closed a few years ago. At the abandoned Fairgrounds there is a large stone monument commemorating the famous stallion, Stonewall King. I'm surprised that some S.O.B. who is offended by stud horses hasn't petitioned to have that monument removed. We have one new Commissioner now, so maybe the vote wouldn't be unanimous. I've lived in Boone County all of my life, and it seems like the assholes and the idiots are getting thicker all the time.

Stonewall King Monument at the abandoned Boone County Fairgrounds. It's looking kind of shabby since the Fairgrounds closed.

*   *   *   *   *

When Marcia and I moved to our farm in 1963 the bridge east of our house was too narrow to cross with anything that had any size to it: Cars, trucks, tractors without duels, and two row machinery could make it O.K., but anything wider than that had to loop around the entire block, about 4 miles out of the way.

There were several bridges around the county at that time that had been de-railed with a cutting torch; on some of them the railings were completely gone, on others they had been partially cut, then heated and bent out from the bridge on a 90° angle. At that time the Boone County Road and Bridge Department (now called Public Works Department) was somewhat flexible, they bent the rules when it suited their purpose. Therefore, I decided to ask them if they might possibly cut the railings off this bridge. I talked to the man who was in charge of the Road Shed in our area and he seemed highly offended that I would even ask such a thing. He informed me that those were safety railings, they had been put there to serve a purpose, and if they cut the railings off it would totally defeat that purpose and they weren't going to do it. Then he went on to say that he didn't want me to do it either. We visited for a few minutes and as I turned to leave he said, "I'm pretty sure we won't have anyone working in that area anytime next week and if the railings would happen to disappear when we're not around there wouldn't be much we could do about it."

The following Monday I took my cutting torch to the bridge and cut the railings off. I cut the angle iron into lengths I could handle and hauled it home and put it with my other shop steel. A month or six weeks later a County Road Truck stopped at the house one morning and two County employees got out. We visited for a little while, then one of them asked me if I knew what happened to the bridge railings. I replied that just looking it appeared like someone had cut them off with a torch. Then they asked if I knew what happened to the angle iron. I said since it wasn't by the bridge whoever cut the railings off must've taken it with them. The County workers told me that was pretty much how it looked to them, then they got in the truck and left and that was the last I ever heard about the bridge railings. I crossed that bridge with machinery and loaded grain trucks for several years, 'til Larry Cook fell through it one day with a lime truck and it was replaced with a big culvert, which has never handled the volume of water that comes down that creek after a big rain. More Boone County engineering genius!

*   *   *   *   *

I really don't need to watch the weather forecast on TV; I just look at the gravel road in front of the house. If the county is grading it and getting lots of fine, dusty gravel spread across the driving area, I know it's going to rain and make a sloppy nasty mess. Actually, I'd rather deal with the slop than the dust. Oscar Elley didn't believe in wasting money, so on the rare occasions when he would have lime spread on his farm he always made the trucks leave 50 yards or so along the road un-limed. He would laugh and say, "The County Road Department limes that for me."

*   *   *   *   *

For several years in the 1980s and 90s the Boone County Public Works Department was on a blacktop binge. They were trying to blacktop every road in the county, but they wanted to put most of the burden on the adjacent landowners. They scheduled a meeting one evening in the Community Room at the BCHS Museum to discuss the black topping of Bearfield Road.

Several elected officials and some engineer with the Road Department made a presentation, the gist of which was "move your fences back 20 feet on each side of the road at your expense, deed the right-of-way to the County and we'll get started on this project almost immediately." They were pretty much met with dead silence. After stuttering and blundering for several minutes they announced that they would be at tables at the back of the room to answer questions.

Mom was well up in her 80s, but she was still sharp as a tack. She couldn't hear too good, and her eyesight was weak, but they weren't going to slip much past her. We walked back to a table where some old fat boy was sitting with a big smile on his face, ready to give us his spiel. I introduced Mom and myself, told him where Mom's property was located, then said "Just so you know where we're coming from, Mom is not donating any right-of-way, if you want it you buy it at full price. Also, she is not spending a dime to move the fence. If the fence is moved, you will build a new woven wire, two barb fence with steel posts every 10 feet, and it will be completed before you remove the old fence." The guy looked at Mom and asked "Mrs. Easley, is that really how you feel about this?" When Mom assured him it was, he kind of waved his hands and said "We just don't understand why you people have that attitude. We run into this everywhere we go." I said, "To begin with I don't like being called 'you people'. With that said, you want us to donate valuable real estate and spend around $6000 per mile to build new fence when we've already got good fence, and you don't understand why we don't jump at the chance? You need to get out of your ivory tower and find out what's going on in the real world."

A couple of months later the county dumped about 3 inches of waste rock on the road, packed it real good and then laid down a layer of blacktop and rolled it in. It's a little narrow, and in places where there were trees on one side, the blacktop is almost against the fence on the other side, but they were determined they were going to build a blacktop road, so for better or worse that's what they did.

*   *   *   *   *

Monroe Lanham owned the farm at the southeast corner of I 70 and Range Line Road for many years, and his grandsons still own it. I started baling hay on his farm in the mid-70s, then raised beans, wheat and milo on it 'til I quit crop farming after 1993. Range Line Road was still a county gravel road at that time. Richard Head Auto Auction was the first commercial business south of I 70 on Range Line. Richard and two or three other people wanted the road black topped. The County agreed to furnish equipment and labor, if adjacent landowners would give right-of-way and pay for the material. Mr. Lanham lived in town and came out to his farm every weekend. One Saturday morning Richard Head showed up at the farm to discuss the proposed road improvements. He eventually told Mr. Lanham that based on the road frontage, his share of the cost would be XX dollars, plus the right-of-way donation. Mr. Lanham replied "What in the hell do you mean my share? My driveway entrance is off of I 70 drive S. E., I don't use that road, I don't need it and I'm not paying for it!" Richard said, "Mr. Lanham if that road was black topped your farm would be worth a lot more money." Mr. Lanham replied "It's worth so much now that no one can afford to buy it, that's why I still own the son of a bitch!

A couple of years later the road finally got black topped, but it was done without Mr. Lanham's help. When he said he wasn't paying for that road he meant it.

*   *   *   *   *

When Bob Baumgartner ran a road grader for Boone County I've seen him drive through Turner Farm Road many times with the blade up. If he found some potholes or a wash-boardy area he would drop the blade and work on it 'til it was in good shape, then he'd go on down the road with the blade up. His theory was "If it's in good shape don't mess with it."

Several years before Bob retired the Road and Bridge Department underwent a management change, and the operators lost the right to think for themselves. Each one of them had a chart on the wall, and they did what the chart said to do despite the fact that it might be really, really stupid! If Bob's chart said grade Turner Farm Road on Feb. 22nd, that's what he did. If the road was frozen solid he let the blade down lightly and scratched over the frozen surface. If it was raining he smeared mud back-and-forth across the road, and if it was dry and the tracks were hard and smooth that didn't matter, he bladed loose gravel and dust across the surface. More than once if Bob saw me he would stop and apologize for making a mess of the road, but it wasn't his fault, the educated idiots were leading the parade.

What's Ours is Theirs

SOME people, and I emphasize SOME, respect other people's property rights. However, there are a hell of a lot of assholes who don't have anything of their own who think they have the right to trespass on or destroy other people's property at any time. Over the years I've dealt with deer hunters, mushroom hunters, picnickers, lovers, thieves, surveyors, plain old idiots, appraisers, and damn hot air balloons. I don't know which is the worst, but I really dislike balloons landing on my property. If a balloon pilot has trouble keeping it up he should carry Viagra with him when he's flying.

*   *   *   *   *

Years ago, when Arno Winkler owned the farm across the road from ours he came over one day during deer season to check his wheat. He noticed tire tracks in the field and followed them to almost the north end of the farm where he discovered a Jeep stuck in the mud. Arno called Boone County Sheriff Charlie Foster, who checked out the Jeep and then had it towed to the impound lot. The next Saturday the Jeep's owner brought some help and came to get his Jeep. When he couldn't find it he called the Sheriff's Department and reported it stolen. He didn't get much sympathy. By the time he paid the wrecker bill, five days in the impound lot, a trespassing fine and settled up with Arno for ruts in the wheatfield, he was one highly pissed off deer hunter. Charlie told him the next time he wanted to drive in someone's field he probably should get permission first. There are a lot of dumb asses around who seem to think it's fun to make ruts on someone else's property, but if something like this happened more often it might change their attitude.

A lot of people in Columbia whined about the "Good Old Boys" system in Boone County, but damn it was nice when Charlie Foster was Sheriff, and Larry McCray, Al Britton and Larry Winfrey were Deputies. If you needed something you could call someone you knew, who actually had a pretty good idea of what was going on out in the country, and usually get something done pretty quick.

*   *   *   *   *

When I was farming the Schwabe Place John would come out occasionally and just wander around for couple of hours. One fall I had finished cutting beans and John had come out for a walk on the first day of deer season. He was about halfway across the big bottom when he heard an engine revving up. He looked up the hill and saw a 4WD truck roaring down across the bean stubble. The truck slid to a stop in a cloud of dust, and a guy in an orange hat and orange vest jumped out. He looked at John and said "What the hell do you think you're doing? This is private property!" John asked, "Really?" The guy replied "Yeah really! This farm belongs to Hazel and John Schwabe, I take care of it for them, and they don't allow any damn trespassers!"

John stuck out his hand and said, "I'd like to introduce myself, my name is John Schwabe." The guy stood there for a moment with a stunned look on his face, then shook John's hand, smiled and said, "Hello John, I was just trying to look after your interest." John said "Thank you, but I'll look after them myself. You need to leave now."

The guy left, but there's no doubt in my mind he was back in his tree stand the next morning.

*   *   *   *   *

One Saturday morning back in the '80s I had overlooked the fact that it was opening day of deer season. About an hour after daylight, I pulled into the big bottom on the Schwabe Place with a tractor and plow. I dropped the plow and headed across the field. By the time I got to the North end, turned, and started back, six people in orange vests and hats had come down out of tree stands by the creek. I'd bet that none of them knew the others were there. If several deer had come out of the brush at the same time it would have sounded like a war zone. So much for John's "NO TRESPASSING."

*   *   *   *   *

In September 2017 I attended the Heritage Festival which was held at Nifong Park and the Boone County Historical Society Museum. I had my 1950 Dodge pickup on display, and Richard Sorrels was showing his 1914 International truck. We had a couple of lawn chairs and were relaxing and visiting with anyone who came along and wanted to talk. We had been chasing the shade, and we were probably 30 to 40 yards from our trucks. I happened to glance toward my truck and saw a 10- or 12-year-old boy standing on the rear fender. A woman I assume was his mother was standing there watching him. As I started toward the truck she could tell by my expression I wasn't happy, and when I got close enough she asked, "Is it all right if he climbs on the truck?" I said "On the paint, with his feet? Hell no it's not all right!" She said "Oh" in a very offended tone of voice, then motioned the boy down. I don't know what in the hell she was thinking about, letting that kid do that. It's actually hard to imagine there's a grown woman around who is so rude, inconsiderate and just plain old stupid that she would let her kid climb on someone's antique vehicle with his damn feet, but I know there's at least one of them out there, 'cause I talked to the dumb bitch!

* * * * *

Steve Crowley told me that after Melissa (his wife) read my second book she remarked "Alan is kind of blunt sometimes, isn't he?" Melissa, it's for damn sure no one ever accused me of being subtle, especially not when some dumb bitch lets her kid climb around on my truck with his shoes.

* * * * *

When the city of Columbia was preparing to run the Clear Creek branch of their sewer line back in the early 1980s, they had a real asshole surveyor running the initial route. I don't know his name or who he worked for, but he was a real prick.

No one had contacted Mom for permission to come on the farm, so one afternoon when I was checking cattle I was surprised to see a line of grade stakes running across the farm with elevations marked on them with a sharpie. No permission, no stakes, so I pulled them up. A couple of days later they were back. Same results. The next time I was there the stakes were back. I was busily pulling them up when I heard someone holler, and saw a guy heading towards me as fast as a fat man can run on a hot day. When he asked me what I thought I was doing I replied that some dumb son-of-a-bitch had driven sticks in the ground on my Mother's farm, and I was pulling them up. He said, "Those are survey stakes!" I replied,

"Well, in that case some dumb son-of-a-bitch has driven survey stakes into the ground on my mother's farm, but since the dumb prick didn't ask permission to come on the farm I'm pulling them up." He indignantly told me that he didn't need permission, that surveyors could go anywhere they needed to go when conducting a survey. I never did check to see if that was actually a law, or just some of his dumb bullshit, but I told him whether he needed permission or not he'd better get it if he wanted his stakes to remain in place. I told him the ones already driven were coming up, since they were driven without permission, but that if he'd leave and get permission from Mom before he came back I'd leave them alone from then on, but otherwise I'd pull them up as fast as his fat ass could drive them.

He wasn't happy about it, but he left and called Mom and got permission to do his thing. After that the stakes pretty much stayed in place except for a few the cows knocked down, and one or two that I might have accidentally run over with my truck while I was driving around checking cattle.

*   *   *   *   *

Nick Leslie and Greg went to Rock Bridge High School together and have remained friends over the years. Nick is one of the very few people other than family members who has permission to hunt on the farm on Bearfield Road.

Nick has deer hunted there for years and usually has one or two deer stands in place at all times. A few years ago, he had left a stand set up in the Catalpa thicket on the east side of the farm. A couple of weeks before deer season he drove over to check his stand, but it was gone. There were tire tracks near the tree, fairly narrow, like would have been made by a big side-by-side four-wheeler or an older Jeep. He followed the tracks to the northeast corner of the farm, where he found the fence cut. The tracks continued onto the Phillips farm, then turned north towards the trailer park. Shortly before reaching the trailer park he discovered his deer stand set up in the edge of the woods, on land that used to belong to Woodhaven Home. Nick took the stand down and tacked a note on the tree with his name and phone number, then a short message; "You stole my deer stand, I wasn't done with it so I took it back, I recommend you don't come looking for it." Nick patched the fence when he went back through and that was the last of that little episode.

It's hard to imagine someone stealing a deer stand and setting it back up within walking distance of where they stole it. They either had hellish big balls, or a really serious case of STUPID!

*   *   *   *   *

Shortly after Elvin Sapp bought the Phillips Farm Nick Leslie was scouting for deer one afternoon on Mom's place when he spotted someone wandering around in the pasture.

Nick walked over to him and said that he was on private property, and he needed to leave. The man told Nick he was Elvin Sapp and that he was looking for a location for a new street. Nick said "I don't care if you're Jesus Christ, you're trespassing on Easley property and you need to get your ass off now! Build your damn street on the other side of the fence." Elvin called me that night and apologized for not asking permission to come on the farm, and we got along fine the whole time he was developing the Phillips property. I've known Elvin for years, and I've always had a lot of respect for him. He's one of the most honest developers who ever hit Boone County.

*   *   *   *   *

One of the most interesting trespass stories I ever heard occurred on Monroe Lanham's farm at the corner of I-70 and Rangeline Road. Mr. Lanham and his wife were out of state on vacation one summer, and while they were gone someone moved in the little house on the farm and took up residence for a few days. Shortly after they got back Mr. Lanham went out to the farm one morning. He soon called me and asked if I had seen any activity around his house while they were gone. Since the wheat was cut and the beans were too big to cultivate I had not had any reason to stop at the farm, and the house is far enough from the road that you would really have to look hard to notice anything out of the way, so therefore I'd seen nothing. He asked me if I had time to run up to the farm for a few minutes. By the time I got there the Sheriff's Department had already been and gone, but what had happened was pretty plain, and since no real harm was done it was almost amusing.

There was a stove in the kitchen of the old house, and Mr. Lanham always kept dishes, cooking utensils, a supply of canned goods and crackers and whatever else he thought he might need to fix a meal. The padlock had been prized off the back door, and just inside on the back porch was a wastebasket about half full of empty food cans and paper towels. On the kitchen table was a stack of plates, cups, serving bowls, silverware and cooking pots, all freshly washed. The bedroom window was open and a box fan had been hung in front of it to pull cool air into the house.

The padlock had also been prized off the door of the storage shed in the backyard, and the new tenant had figured out which electric breaker turned on the deep well pump so that he had running water in the house. He also found some number nine smooth wire in the shed and put up a 20-foot-long clothesline between the trees. Apparently he had done his laundry in the bathtub and hung it out to dry.

He forgot to shut the bedroom window before he left, so if it had rained the bedroom floor might've gotten a little wet, but he pretty much took care of everything else. He found clean bed linens in the closet and made the bed, and he washed, dried and folded the ones he had used, and left them stacked on the foot of the bed. He left the clothesline up, but he cleaned up any mess he had made, turned off the electricity to the well pump, and closed the doors to the house and shed before he left. The only thing he actually stole was the food that he ate and the soap he used to do the dishes and laundry, plus a couple of bars of hand soap that he took with him when he left.

The Sheriff's Department surmised that he was a hitchhiker on I-70 who had stopped for a handout, and when he discovered all of the padlocks he decided to take a chance and rest up a little. They estimated he had spent three nights and two days at the house. Mr. Lanham said he had seen invited guests who caused more trouble and made a bigger mess than this guy did.

Emily's Memories

Author's Note:

Emily K. (Short) Wisley was raised on a farm just south of the Gans Bridge on Highway 63, about 2 miles from our house if you cut across the fields at an angle. I was a year ahead of her in school. We attended Little Bonne Femme Church, Grindstone School, and Hickman High School together. Emily attended nursing school, then moved out of the state, and the only time I've seen her since High School was at her dad's funeral several years ago.

After the funeral I gave Emily a copy of my first book for old times' sake. When my second book was published her cousin, Sue Baumgartner, asked me to send Emily a copy. Shortly afterwards I received a long letter from Emily with questions, comments and memories. After reading it several times I decided it would fit right in my third (and last) book, so I wrote and asked if she would mind if I printed the letter. She graciously gave me permission to use "Emily's Memories"

January 29, 2018

Hello Alan,

Thank you so much for the copy of "It Sure 'Nuff Happened!" I have enjoyed reading both of your books and even recognized some of the characters and events. You must have enjoyed putting them together and chuckling over old memories. Some of the stories brought a tear to me so they must have had a big impact on you. The trips down memory lane in your books led me to call my sister Marilyn in Colorado to talk about old times.

We lived on a farm on Highway 63 about five miles from Columbia. Living on the highway led to a number of stories. People would see the very visible farm gas tank and suddenly need gas which Daddy often supplied. It was amazing how many people needed gas at that section of highway. I don't know if there was a speed limit on that highway but there was lots of speeding and certainly no seat belts, blinkers or air bags. Remember hand signals?

Sometime in the early 1950s, the KOMU TV station was built near us. In 1955 Red Foley did fourteen broadcasts from the station. Marilyn and I would run down the graveled driveway and wait at the side of the highway for him to drive by on his way to the station. As I remember, he was in a gold Cadillac and we were so impressed.

In the late 1940's we would fairly often have hobos knock on the door needing a handout. One morning, Marilyn was refusing to eat her breakfast fried egg when a knock came. Mother slapped Marilyn's egg between two slices of bread and passed it out the door. Then, there was a stunned Marilyn with less breakfast. There was some concern that the house had been marked in some way to indicate that one could get food handed out the door there.

Sometimes, the happenings were more troublesome. Once, a man came walking across a field and asked my father for water from the pump. Daddy handed him a dipper full of water. The man silently walked over to our dog, poured the water over the dog's head, dropped the dipper and without another word walked on. In later years, there was the time that Marilyn and I were home alone late in the afternoon and heard one of the horses making a lot of noise. Through the growing dusk, we could see a man with a bridle trying to get the horse to cooperate. That horse could only be bridled by Daddy, and we peeped from the darkened house until we could no longer see him. He was gone when our parents came home and the horse was still there. We had no idea who he was or where he went.

As to Bonne Femme church, we remember potluck dinners sometimes held outside after morning services. It was often very hot and people used "funeral home" cardboard fans attached to a wooden paddle to move some air. After that, the people would pull their food out of the hot cars and set it out on tables under a tree to share. There were ice cream socials in summer evenings with each family bringing their hand cranked freezers with various flavors (peach, strawberry, etc.) to share. As night closed in, the kids would scare each other when playing hide and seek among the tombstones at the back of the church.

There are so many things that one wouldn't expect to see today. Do you remember plugging watermelon? I know that I have been with Daddy at Walkup's store and watching him take a plug out of a watermelon to see if it was good enough to buy. What happened to the rejected plugged melons?

In 1955, I had pneumonia and the doctor actually made home visits to give me injections of penicillin in the buttocks - speaking of plugged melons. Very embarrassing to a twelve-year-old.

Then there were the party line telephones. I don't remember how many homes were on our line but at least four. Our ring was 4 shorts - and you always assumed someone else was listening in. Perhaps someone else had one long ring, two shorts and one long. We could say "So and so has a call" - and listen in if we wanted. Or we could just pick up and listen to see if anyone was talking after making an outgoing call.

Certainly, the radio was vital. I couldn't wait to get home from school for the Lone Ranger on weekdays. Marilyn loved Big John and Sparky. I tried to never miss a St. Louis Cardinals game and remember trading baseball cards with you. I sure wish I had those cards now. Today I'm a Yankee fan and those games on TV are no more exciting than the Cardinals games on radio with Harry Caray announcing and Stan Musial at the plate.

Also, there were many things that happened in the one room schools that you would never see today. There were the periodic visits of the mobile x-ray van. We would all be lined up and sent in (I'm guessing no parental permission) for a chest x-ray in the hunt for tuberculosis. Who knows the level of radiation in that day? I still have black spots on my knees from falling on cinders that were used in front of Grindstone and on the paths to the outhouses.

I don't remember talk of playground safety either. There was no kindergarten and I think only an eight month school year. It was a privilege to be able to go outside and clean the erasers of chalk by banging them together - I'm fairly certain that would be an invitation to an asthma attack today. There weren't tissues that I remember but a sodden handkerchief from home when one had a cold. Did we wash our hands? I remember taking pint jars of milk to school. Was it refrigerated? Was there a phone at the school? Or did the teacher have to go next door to make an emergency call? Certainly, there was no special education and I remember one hyperactive boy being tied into his seat one day. Can you imagine what fire safety would say about that now? Do kids now still play Red Rover or Annie Over? I remember loving Annie Over and wonder how it was played - is there a rule book somewhere? Thank goodness, we didn't play Dodge Ball - that was a horror waiting for going into Jefferson Junior and Hickman High. And then there was the field trip to the Missouri State Prison in Jefferson City. We actually walked through a cell block to stare at the prisoners. Marilyn remembers being frightened as some of the prisoners reached through the bars. Can you imagine that happening now with grade school students?

One of our chief complaints was having to wear dresses even in the coldest weather. Only if the temperature was zero degrees, were we allowed to put on "leggin's" in order to get to school but then we had to take them off. I do think it must have been extremely challenging to teach eight grades in one room with no teacher's aide and no accommodation for special needs. Did we even recognize special needs then? I seem to remember that 5th and 6th grades and 7th and 8th grades being grouped in some way - so that something like history would be taught one year to the combined group at the 5th and 7th level and then at the 6th and 8th level the following year. I don't know how that would work if someone moved or ended up getting the information 6th then 5th then 8th then 7th.

I only know that somehow most of us came out with a basic education and not enough appreciation for the teacher who kept it under control. I do know that I had to study agriculture in 7th grade - it must have been assumed we would all be farmers or wives of farmers. I remember learning about crop rotation, how to plow a hill, breeds of cattle, etc. think it was a state curriculum for rural students.

Now comes one of the real issues and that concerns being a girl. I loved playing softball and because we were such a small school there weren't enough students to make up two teams unless the girls played too - so we played. And then the consolidated New Haven was built and now there were enough boys to make up the two teams. Instantly, girls could be a cheering group for the boys. What is saddest is that we didn't even know that this was a problem - it was "just how it was", no questions asked.

Later when I was in Hickman High school and playing basketball, girls were not allowed to run the whole court. We could only run to the midcourt line and wait for the ball to get back to our end. Apparently, girls were too delicate to run full court. However, we could stand in our bare legs and be blasted by some Amazon in Dodge Ball - I still can feel the bruises.

The school bus was always an experience. Marilyn remembers, before consolidation, that the black kids always sat in the back. I don't know if this was mandated or just "the way it was". I think that after consolidation of the one room schools and integrated classrooms that the school bus seating was based on who got to the seat first.

Even though I had one year at New Haven with only seventh and eighth grades in one room, the move to ninth grade at Jefferson Junior in Columbia was quite a shock. We were the country kids bused into a school where most students had already been together for two years and knew how to do such things as have a homeroom, change classrooms all day, go to gym, not recess, have classes based on perceived ability, etc.

But the incident I most remember happened in preparation for going into the "big city" school. Those of us in eighth grade at New Haven had to go into Columbia to take tests so that our ability could be perceived. New Haven's consolidation of one room schools included the "colored" school. Our eighth grade New Haven group included one quiet, rather shy, black boy and when the testing broke for lunch we went to the Gem Drug Store to eat. As the group of us were just settled in our chairs, a waitress came over and told that student that they didn't serve colored, and he would have to leave. Most of us sat there stunned but Bobby Forsee got up and left with him. I think that is the first time that the ugliness of segregation really hit home for me and I will always respect Bobby, at about age fourteen, for quickly perceiving what was happening and the courage to act in support of a fellow student. That was the true ability.

Your books are obviously written from a male perspective - so there are some "olden" things I will mention from a female point of view. Bullying is not new to either sex, but girls did it in a passive-aggressive way. I remember one girl in the one room school who somehow became the "leader of the pack". She would quietly pass the word each day as to who was "out" and for that day the rest of we girls would shun that girl. The next day it would be someone else's turn to be "it". I remember living in fear of being the chosen one (which of course happened) and trying desperately to stay on the good side of this bully. One time four girls were selected to go somewhere to sing for a group. The bully quietly passed the word that three of us would wear gray sweaters and green skirts and not tell the fourth girl who showed up in navy blue and white. I'm still ashamed of participating in that. We were young and seemed not to realize that we were allowing this manipulative behavior to continue. Yes, girls can be mean and I can't imagine how much more traumatizing it is now with the internet.

Of course, we continued to wear dresses or skirts of appropriate length through high school. don't remember if there was a rule about dress if the temperature was zero or below. We were too busy torturing ourselves in other ways to worry about the cold. For example, there were girdles. We actually wore girdles at the time of our life when we had firm bodies. We attached our hose/ nylons to the girdle or else wore a garter belt. These stockings had seams up the back and it was imperative to keep the seams straight. What a relief to get out of this garb. Then there was the period of time when we wore layers of starched petticoats to hold our skirts wide. Marilyn and I spent a lot of time starching these circular petticoats and draping them over parallel clothes lines to get as much underskirt puff as possible. And somewhere along the line were saddle shoes that needed constant maintenance.

Finally, I will mention brush rollers for a lovely hair do. We actually wound our hair over the wire rollers with stiff bristles and secured them with long plastic pins (that could pierce the skull) before going to bed and trying to sleep. Fashion makes sheep of us all.

Thanks Alan for the trip down memory lane. I noticed you mentioned Conrad Stawski in your second book. He was one of my favorite teachers of all time. I still remember things that he said in English class. One day, he was explaining that the purpose of language was to communicate, and one should not criticize people just because of incorrect grammar. "If a truck driver says, 'I don't want none of them there goddammed potatoes' you know exactly what he means and he has communicated effectively." He also wrote his sperm count on the board one day and that was quite interesting since I didn't even know that sperm had a count and I'm sure he did it for shock value - unless he was bragging. He was not only an effective teacher but always interesting. In fact, he told us that - "be interesting". You've nailed that with your books.

   - Emily K. (Short) Wisley

7th and 8th grade class at the Old Carlisle School, after Grindstone burned. 1956.

Back Row: Emily Short, Nina Dirskmeyer, Alan Easley, J.E. Rich, Tom Ripppeto

Front Row: Marilyn Elder, Claude (Sonny) Weldon

Holidays in the Country

For Marcia.
1943-2012

She loved the holidays.

When Sis and I were little kids our cousin, John Easley, used to bring fireworks out to the farm on July 4th. The only fireworks we ever had were a few sparklers, so an older cousin bringing real fireworks was a pretty big deal.

One year everyone was sitting south of the house and John was lighting the goodies by the garden fence. He poked a big hole in the side of a quart syrup can and tossed a cherry bomb inside. It made a hell of a good explosion, but afterwards he couldn't find the can. The next morning when Pappy went to feed the hogs he found half of the can by the corn crib west of the barn. That was at least 50 yards from where the cherry bomb went off. It's a good thing that the can went south instead of north, or someone might've lost their head. We never did find the rest of the can.

*   *   *   *   *

I never really enjoyed dressing up at Halloween, but despite that we had some pretty good Halloween parties when I attended the one room country school. We always had the obligatory contests; best costume, worse costume, prettiest, etc., but after the costumes came off is when the fun began. There were always dishes full of that nasty candy corn setting around, and lots of other much better treats. We would bob for apples, and there were always two or three kids with snot running down their upper lips who would do a pretty good job of washing it off in the tub of water as they tried to bite into an apple. The health department would really love that now! When you think about it, it was pretty nasty. I guess we wanted an apple so bad that we just didn't think about it.

There were games and songs, and Channing Crane who lived on the next farm south of us, always wound up playing the piano. I don't know if he was any good or not, but he would pound the hell out of it and everyone apparently enjoyed listening. While this was going on some of the older boys always slipped out and tipped the outhouses over, then took the entrance gate off its hinges and hoisted it onto the roof of the school or hid it in the brush on Dr. Nifong's farm.

I didn't enjoy tipping the outhouses as much as some of the other boys did, because Pappy was on the School Board, and before the next school day I always got to help him, Hale Cavcey, and sometimes Paul Short set them back over the pit. But the gate was a different story. Mrs. Moreau would smile and give us a couple of hours out of class to "See if you can find the school yard gate, someone carried it off on Halloween." She never bothered to send anyone who didn't know where the gate was hidden. She always knew exactly who had done it.

*   *   *   *   *

For several years on Halloween I would take the Olivet Church Youth Group on a hayride. One year when Greg and Jeff were in Junior High I had plowed all day at Leroy Sapp's before the hayride. I got home just before dark, unhitched the plow and installed the drawbar, then drove to the church and hitched on to the hay wagon that I had left there earlier.

Someone else was taking a load of little kids and parents, and I had mostly Junior High kids. The kids finally got loaded and we headed out. I hadn't much more than pulled onto the road when someone yelled "STOP." I looked back and the wagon was sitting in the road. I hadn't gotten the spring-pin locked in place and the drawbar had come out. Luckily I found the pin, and laid down in the middle of the gravel road and reinstalled the drawbar, making sure that the pin was locked in place this time.

About half of those kids had already snuggled down under the hay and were so interested in what they were doing that they didn't even know the wagon had stopped. If we had sat in the middle of the road for the next hour and a half they would've been just as happy as if they were riding.

*   *   *   *   *

Turner Vemer never was very easy on equipment, and his old I. H. pickup took a beating. One year a few days before Thanksgiving Turner was headed east on Bowling Lane when a flock of wild turkeys started across the road. He said "Easley, I thought there goes my Thanksgiving dinner." He sped up, with the idea of running over a turkey. Just before he got to them the last two turkeys left the ground, and he smacked them with the front of the truck instead of the bumper. He had two turkeys for Thanksgiving, but he had to buy a new headlight, grill and radiator. He said "Easley, I probably should have just gone to the store and bought a turkey."

*   *   *   *   *

I made it 75 years without taking part in the after Thanksgiving "Black Friday" sales, but in 2017 I finally saw something that made it worth going to town with all those idiots. Actually, I waited 'til Saturday so traffic wasn't quite so bad, and I went to Tractor Supply Company instead of the Mall, so that culled out about 95% of the gawkers and it was worth the trip. Plus, I saved $300 on a nice gun safe. I can't think of anything else that I might possibly ever need, so thankfully I won't have to do it again. Shopping is kind of like cutting thorn sprouts on a 90° day; I can do it if I have to, but I'd just as soon not.

Happy Birthdays!

Greg's 3rd birthday. Jeff and Greg, Grandpa Wilkie and Pappy in back. May 1966.

Marcia's 40th birthday at Blackwell's. January 1983.

Justin and Momma on her 91st birthday. "Grandma Easley" to everyone except me and Sis. April 2000.

My 74th birthday. Kristin Kijowski, Stephen, me, and Jamie. They put candles on my birthday pecan pie. July 2016.

*   *   *   *   *

Christmas, 1953; When I was 11 years old I figured I was plenty big enough to have my own gun, and I wasn't bashful about dropping hints. However, Pappy apparently thought I needed a little more time.

When we had cut firewood that fall I did all I could do with a full-sized double-bit axe, but it was almost too much for me to handle. I had seen a long package under the tree with my name on it, so Christmas morning I eagerly opened what I thought was my new rifle. It was all I could do not to show my disappointment when it turned out to be a short-handled pole axe (single bit), small enough for me to easily use. Of all the Christmas presents I opened when I was a kid that was the only one I really remember, mainly because of what it wasn't.

When my birthday rolled around in July I got a nice, single shot, Remington .22 rifle. The axe disappeared over the years, but I still have that rifle and I always will. Things have a way of working themselves out.

*   *   *   *   *

When I was in grade school the kids always put on some kind of Christmas program; The little kids would do a few short skits, and the upper grades would present a somewhat longer play, then Bill Menteer would show up dressed as Santa. Of my eight years at Grindstone there is only one Christmas that really stands out in my mind.

I don't remember what year it was, but it was before Grindstone burned so I was probably in the fifth or sixth grade. That was a totally different era, and for our play that year we were all made up in blackface. I was the "Cool Dude." I wore blue jeans, a suit coat, neck-tie, a black derby hat that had been borrowed from someone, and I had a big red flower in my lapel that was hooked to a squeeze bottle in my pocket so that I could squirt anyone who upset me. I was reared back and putting on a show.

The only problem was I forgot my lines. Shortly after the play started I drew a blank, the only line I could remember should've been spoken about two thirds of the way through the play, but that's what I remembered, so that's what I said. Whoever was on stage with me picked up on the next line and we continued on. It wound up being one of the shortest Christmas plays ever put on at Grindstone School.

*   *   *   *   *

One other Christmas that's easy to remember occurred after most of the grandkids were in their early teens. Cordless drills were just starting to become popular, and Marcia had mentioned a couple of times that she'd like to have one in the house so she wouldn't have to go to the shed to get my drill and an extension cord every time she wanted to drill a hole for something.

I was working for MFA in Boonville at the time, and in early December Snoddy's Store had gotten a shipment of industrial grade drill bits. They were packed in heavy brown paper bags, with a couple of dozen assorted sizes of bits in each bag. Steve Crowley and I had bought some for the Fertilizer Plant and they were right decent bits, so I got a package of them for Marcia. Then I bought a nice cordless drill with a charger, packed in a hard case.

We have a tradition of opening one present at a time on Christmas, so everyone can enjoy each other's presents. I made sure Marcia got the drill bits first, and after she un-wrapped them she smiled real big, then asked "Now what am I supposed to do with industrial-strength drill bits?" Her next present answered that question, and after she opened it she smiled real big again and then gave me a present from her. It wasn't the same brand, but it was a nice battery powered drill with charger, packed in a hard case. Greg, Jamie and the grandkids were having trouble trying to keep from laughing. I could see the humor in Marcia and I exchanging drills, but I didn't think it was quite that funny, until Greg handed me a present from him and Jamie. It was a battery powered drill with charger, packed in a hard case!

I don't remember what anyone else got that Christmas, but opening all of those cordless drills sure made a fun memory.

*   *   *   *   *

Last year just before Christmas I bought six new feed sacks from MFA. I peeled the printed outside layer off and used it to wrap presents. Actually, the sacks cost more than wrapping paper would have, but not everyone gets presents wrapped in a feed sack; It sorta adds a little class to the pile under the tree.

*   *   *   *   *

It seems like it hasn't been but a couple of months since I went to Greg and Jamie's for Christmas, but Jamie called me this morning and invited me for Thanksgiving dinner next week. Damn, time sure goes faster than it used to.

*   *   *   *   *

Christmas is Always Fun!

Uncle Edward, Aunt Mary, and Pappy. Christmas, 1977.

Jeff, Marcia, Greg, and me. Christmas, 1977.

Jeff and Justin. Christmas, 1986.

Marcia always had a pretty Christmas tree. Christmas, 1986.

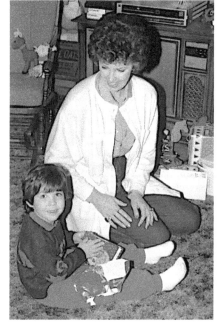

Justin and Marcia. Christmas, 1987.

Matthew Wilkerson and Marcia. Christmas, 1986.

Marcia. Christmas, 2003.

Me. Christmas, 2003.

Momma and Jeff. Christmas, 2003.

Jean. Christmas, 2003.

Sammy and Jean. Christmas, 2003.

Christmas Eve, 2017; Five years ago tonight Marcia and I went to Greg and Jamie's to eat supper and open presents. The family was all there, and we had a good old time. It was Marcia's last Christmas, she passed away December 29, 2012. Damn, damn, damn!

*   *   *   *   *

Early on December 26, 2017, my cell phone rang and when I answered a very professional sounding male voice asked, "May I speak to Marcia please?" I told him he was way behind, because Marcia had been dead for five years. He replied "Oh, I'm so sorry." I said "Yeah, me too!" And then hung up before the S.O.B. could say anything else.

*   *   *   *   *

Years ago, when I had my knee replaced Marcia was still working at Westminster College in Fulton, so we talked Stephen into spending part of his summer vacation as Paw-Paw's nursemaid. Two or three days after I got home from the hospital a physical therapist started coming to the house three days per week. One of the exercises she had me do was the butt squeeze which is exactly what it sounds like. Anytime I was relaxing in my recliner I was supposed to squeeze my butt cheeks together and hold for a count of 10, then do it again. I worked up to 25 or 30 at a time, two or three times a day. One afternoon Stephen was watching me when he suddenly said, "Paw-Paw, if you keep on doing those you'll be able to crack walnuts with your butt!" I said he was probably right, then pretty much forgot about it for a while.

It turned out to be a really good walnut year, so later that fall when I was over at Mom's checking my cows I bunched up a lot of walnuts in the barn lot and ran back and forth over them with the truck, busting the hulls. A few days later I peeled the hulls off and took the nuts home, then laid them out to dry.

Just before Christmas I cracked enough nuts to fill a 36-ounce plastic coffee can and wrapped it in Christmas paper. When he opened his present, on top of the nuts was a note "Merry Christmas, Stephen. I cracked these walnuts just special for you! Paw-Paw." I never did ask Stephen if he picked those nuts out and ate them, or just fed them to the squirrels, but I know what I'd of done!

*   *   *   *   *

Christmas season, 2017, I came home from town one afternoon and discovered that the Fed Ex man had left a 50-inch flatscreen TV on my front porch. Stephen and Kristin, bless their hearts, had gotten tired of watching me squint at a 38-year-old 21-inch T. V. Now comes the fun part, moving a 500-pound entertainment center and an antique TV out of the house to make room for the new one. I bet we can do it. We eventually did, and damn it's nice!

*   *   *   *   *

It's sort of a tradition in our family that all of the Christmas presents get passed out before any of them get opened. That way everyone gets to see who got what. After they're all distributed the youngest person in the room opens a present, and it works up by age from there.

This past Christmas (2020), after the presents had been passed out, my Daughter-in-law, Jamie, said "Ruby gets to open one first because she's the baby, then Rhett, then Lexi, then Lennox." About that time 5-year-old Lexi said, "And Great Paw-Paw opens his last, 'cause he's REALLY OLD."

Whatever

Most stories fit nicely in one category or another, but there are always a few oddballs that have to be dealt with. After I got the rest of the chapters pretty well laid out, whatever was left went here. It's pretty much a hodge-podge of topics, strung out over the years.

*   *   *   *   *

On December 30, 2017, Greg and I cured some hams that we bought from the MU Meat Department. There weren't enough trimmings to make it worthwhile getting the grinder out, so Greg went to Moser's grocery store and bought 25 pounds of trimmings and two pork butts. That made it worthwhile, so on December 31 we ground, seasoned, mixed and bagged 40 pounds of sausage. Nick Leslie came out and  helped, and we had a regular assembly line going. It's a good thing Nick was there, because seeing as how it was five below outside and only 20° in the shed, we didn't really want to spend a whole lot of extra time on that project.

We used Grandpap's old seasoning recipe that goes back to the late 1800s. It will be good sausage, but it's mighty lean, probably gonna have to melt some lard in the skillet to make it fry. Way too much fat has been bred off of hogs over the years, what's called a fat hog today isn't my idea of a fat hog. It would take a hell of a lot of those skinny things to get enough fat to cook up a big kettle of lard.

I fried up a skillet full of the new sausage for supper that night, and lean are not it was pretty damn good eating.

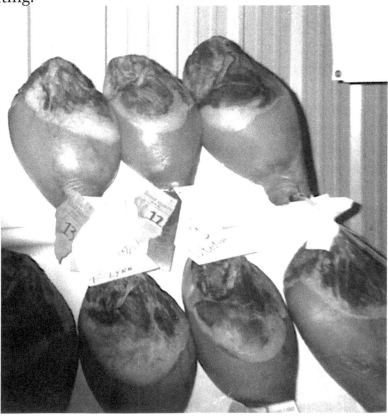

Country hams at the 2008 Boone County Fair.

*   *   *   *   *

Pork Sausage Seasoning

Edward Everett Easley

Two each 3 gallons of ground meat take 2/3 cup of salt, 1/2 cup black pepper, 1/2 teaspoon of cayenne pepper, and 1 tablespoon sage. Mix well. Add to the ground meat and mix thoroughly. Note: a little extra cayenne pepper and a little extra sage won't hurt anything.

*   *   *   *   *

Marcia always loved flowers, so it wasn't very long after we finished building our house 'til she had bunches and bunches of flowers scattered around the yard.

At some point she joined a Lawn and Garden Club that met once a month and toured two or three members homes before settling in somewhere for coffee and snacks. One Sunday afternoon our house was on the tour. It had rained the night before, so I was nesting in the basement with a good book. They started in the front yard, then came through the house as Marcia showed them her plants and decorations. Then they came down the stairs and out the basement door to the backyard.

Marcia gave me a "Hi Babe" as she passed through, and a few of the women acknowledged me, but to most of them I was just another piece of furniture. As the last two stragglers went by I heard one of them remark "I had no idea there were nice houses like this way out here in the country." After they went out the door I thought "Lady you're not just fat and ugly, you're also dumb as hell," but for Marcia's sake I kept my thoughts to myself.

*   *   *   *   *

Marcia used to have flowerbeds scattered around the entire yard, and something was nearly always blooming. After she passed away I pretty much let the flowers go to hell. For the past couple of years Stephen's "more than just a girlfriend," Kristin Kijowski, has done lots and lots of work to bring the flowerbeds back to life. The yard looks nice again, and I really appreciate it.

*   *   *   *   *

When Roger Gilbert was manager of MFA in Columbia, for some reason he didn't want to open early to unload grain trucks during harvest season. Several farmers, myself included, had asked him to consider opening at 7 AM so we could unload, get back to the field, service our combines and be ready to cut when the dew dried off. He made it pretty clear to us that he had no intention of opening earlier.

One fall we had an Advisory Board meeting just as harvest was getting underway. I don't remember who all was on the Board but two or three of us, I'm pretty sure Paul Wayne Garrett was one, cornered Charlie Shauwecker before the meeting and had a little discussion. Charlie was district manager for MFA at the time, and he did more for farmers than anyone in that position, before or since.

When it came time for new business I brought up the subject of early hours during harvest. Roger said "Alan, I've told you before we're not going to open early. If you got unloaded you couldn't get back on Route B with all the rush hour traffic." I replied, "Roger you get my damn truck empty and I'll worry about getting back on Route B!" Two or three other people spoke, and it was starting to get kind of tense, when Charlie raised his hands and stood up. He looked around, then said "Roger, if it will help these gentlemen with their harvest you WILL open at 7 AM, starting tomorrow. As soon as this meeting is over you need to get on the phone and arrange for some people to be here in the morning at 7 AM."

Roger was pissed and he stayed pissed for a while, but none of us really cared what he thought about the situation. MFA was still opening at 7 AM when I quit crop farming after 1993. Organizations like MFA need more employees like Charlie Schauwecker but there's not many of them out there.

*　　*　　*　　*　　*

If you actually need to use a pipe wrench Rigid is the only brand to own. Most of the others are almost hazardous to your health.

With that said, I like to collect antique pipe wrenches. Stillson was the Rigid of its time, they're pretty crude, but they sure beat the competition. Just like companies are now making knockoff Rigid wrenches, companies used to make knockoff Stillson's. If you need information about Stillson wrenches contact Dan Cornell. He definitely knows how to buy them. Dan amassed an impressive Stillson collection in a very short period of time.

Some of the old wrenches have a brand name on them and others were so poorly designed and built that the manufacturer didn't want you to know who made them. I have 40 some wrenches hanging on one wall of the old coal shed, and it's kind of interesting to look at some of them and wonder what in the hell the designer was thinking about. When Stephen and Kristin were working on the road they brought me several unusual designs from Arkansas and Louisiana.

Antique pipe wrenches.

*   *   *   *   *

One year when I was on the Boone County Oil Co-op Board of Directors, the Board members and our wives met at Jack's Coronado Club in late December for a Christmas meal. I would rather have been at Jimmy's Steakhouse or G&D, but I didn't pick the location.

I ordered steak, baked potato and green beans, and when the waiter brought my meal the plate contained 4 or 5 green beans about 6 inches long that were as hard and stiff as they were when someone picked them. I pushed them to the side and chose to ignore them. However, the waiter couldn't leave well enough alone, he stopped at the table and asked if everything was all right. I replied that it was O.K., but it would be better if he'd bring me a dartboard. He looked puzzled and asked, "A dartboard?" I said "Yes, because if I had a dartboard I believe I could throw these beans and stick them and get them off my plate, but if you expect me to eat them you need to take them back to the kitchen, snap them and put in a pan with some water, bacon grease and half an onion and simmer them until they're done, because I don't intend to break a tooth trying to eat them like this."

From the look he gave me I believe he was thinking about where he'd really like to put those beans but he didn't say a word, he just turned and walked away. Marcia asked "Alan, why did you have to do that?" I replied "Babe he asked. If he'd have kept his mouth shut I'd have just let them lay there, but he asked so I told him."

*   *   *   *   *

At that same meal someone ordered a plate of escargot for appetizers. It was the first time I'd ever tried them. I popped one in my mouth and chewed for probably five minutes, and it was at least three times as big as when I started and it still didn't have a tooth mark on it. There was a vase of flowers on our table, so I dropped that rubber ball into the vase and went back to eating normal food. Don't let that fancy name escargot fool you, it's nothing but a damn snail without its shell. Fish bait.

* * * * *

I suppose selling the family farm is something lots of people have to deal with eventually, but when it's been in the family since the 1840s and you know when it sells it will be developed that makes it a little bit harder. Damn progress anyhow.

The old place is about half gone and I haven't paid a Real Estate Agent yet, but it's kind of a pain in the ass sometimes when you do it yourself. I couldn't have done it without Turner Jones; when he finally retires 20 years from now it's going to leave a big hole in the law profession in Columbia.

* * * * *

You can pretty much shut up a smart ass if you can just think of the right thing to say at the right time. One morning several of us were sitting in James Earl's Parlor drinking coffee. I had on a pair of pretty raggedy overalls, and someone remarked it looked like it was about time to dig up a can of money in the backyard and buy some new britches. I replied, "You probably won't understand what I'm fixing to tell you because you've never had any experience with it, but when I put these on this morning they were brand-new, hard work is what caused this!" That was the last time I heard anything about new britches.

I didn't think any more about that remark, but three months or so later I was out in the driveway one morning when David Grant came down the road and pulled in. I had on a fairly new pair of overalls, and David looked at me and said, "Damn Easley it doesn't look like you've done much work yet this morning."

*　　*　　*　　*　　*

Most of the stories in this book happened reasonably close to Columbia, but after visiting with David Reed from Tipton Missouri one morning, I decided Tipton's not all that far away and I just had to include this story in the book.

I was attending a farm toy show at the Elks Club building on Route WW east of Columbia when I ran into Ron Eggers, who is a member of the Missouri River Valley Steam Engine Association in Boonville, where I'm also a member. Ron introduced me to his friend David Reed from Tipton, Missouri. Larry Pauley from Deer Park was also there, and it soon turned into a good, old-fashioned bull shit session.

David told us that he worked for the shoe factory in Tipton for many years, until they closed to make room for more imported Chinese shoes. His father-in-law had passed away not too long before the factory announced that it would be closing, so David decided since he was going to be out of work he would rent the farm and go into the cattle business.

He told me he went to South Dakota and bought 10 really nice Polled Hereford heifers from a top-notch Hereford breeder, and hauled them to the farm in Tipton. He pampered them, kept them well fed and did all of the necessary veterinary procedures but after three years not a single heifer had calved. He drove to California Missouri one afternoon and talked to the County Extension Agent, who agreed to come out to the farm the next day to see what he could figure out. He arrived the next morning and got in David's pickup and they drove over the entire farm checking pasture conditions, water quality, and looking closely at the heifers. Finally, the agent asked to see the barn. After walking through the barn, he asked David where his bull was. David said "Bull?" The agent told him you have to have bulls if you want to have calves. David sold the heifers and bought 10 bulls and he said, "That was three years ago and I still haven't had any damn calves!" I told you it was a good old-fashioned bull shit session.

*   *   *   *   *

When Grandpap was in his early 60s he got involved in some type of round-robin burial insurance program. There were 500 participants scattered all over the United States, and each time one of them died a notice was sent to the organizer who sent a postcard to all the other members. Then they each one mailed a dollar to the surviving family members. The only problem was it was limited to the original 500 participants.

I guess that worked out okay for the ones who died fairly soon, but Grandpap lived to be 98 years old. Over the years he faithfully mailed out dollar bills whenever he received a notice, but Mom said when Grandpap died they got six one-dollar bills in the mail over the next three months. Add in 493 stamps and envelopes used over the years and it really wasn't a very good investment.

*   *   *   *   *

By 1978 New Haven school had pretty much outgrown itself. It had been added on to two or three times over the years and we needed more room again, but there was nowhere left to go. There wasn't any ground available for purchase next to the school, so the Board made the decision to build a satellite school adjacent to El Chaparral Subdivision, about 3 miles north of New Haven. Ten acres of ground was purchased from Emery Sapp & Sons and a new building was built on the site. It opened in 1979 and was subsequently named Cedar Ridge Elementary School. At that time, it housed grades K through four. Donna Dodge was Principal of the new school.

Eventually New Haven and Cedar Ridge were annexed into the Columbia School District. In 2017 the Columbia School Board decided the building was too small, and nearly obsolete, so instead of adding on they built a new school on Ray and Eva Hinshaw's old farm, now known as the Vineyards subdivision. When Cedar Ridge was built in 1978 – 79 El Chaparral was a nice subdivision, but it has backslid over the years and now drug busts and shootings are not uncommon near the school. I'm sure that factored into Columbia's decision to move the school east to the Vineyards. At least they did retain the name, Cedar Ridge.

On May 6, 2018, there was a reunion at the school of past teachers, staff, parents and students. Zane Dodge

New Haven School Board 1979. Left to right: Ken Holland, Turner Vemer, Bill Blackwell, Alan Easley, Gene Nichols (Principal), Betty Baysinger, Milt Miller.

gave a short presentation about Donna's time at the school, and I saw several teachers I hadn't seen since I helped hire them when I was on the New Haven School Board in the late 1970s and early 80s. It was an enjoyable afternoon, but I really hate to see the little school turn into office space for the Columbia School District. It seems like we were keep losing little bits of the past every day.

Damn Virus!

    I was born and raised in Boone County and have lived here all of my life. I've seen some weird shit over the years, but this is about as weird as it gets.

    Chris Campbell at the Boone County Historical Society suggested that people keep a sort of a diary during the pandemic, or as one of my friends calls it, "The DamPanic." I did it for a while, and it was pretty much the same old crap every day, so I quit, I don't want to bore people too much.

April 15, 2020 –

I was 77 years old when this crap hit Boone County. I washed my hands so damn many times that my gloves were two sizes too big. But there wasn't a hell of a lot else that could be done; Wash your hands, swallow a teaspoon full of turpentine occasionally, wear one of those dumb-assed masks when you were out in public, and pray.

When the virus hit I had been retired from MFA for several years and I had sold the last of my cattle a few years earlier, so I didn't have any reason to get out much. However, that doesn't mean that I didn't want to get out. My Daughter-in-law Jamie is a nurse at the VA Hospital, and she was almost paranoid about the virus. She didn't think I had any reason to leave the farm, but since she knew I would anyhow she brought me a mask and I promised to wear it when I was in town. When she'd see my truck on the road she would call me later and say "Pops, I saw your truck, WHERE were you going?" When I'd reply the grocery store, hardware store, lumberyard or wherever, I could almost see her shaking her head over the phone. She'd say, "We could do that for you," and I'd reply, "Thanks, but I really need to get out anyway."

Zane Dodge and I both like toy tractors, and we had started making a toy run occasionally, eating lunch somewhere while we were out, and just generally enjoying ourselves. The virus stopped that, all of the antique shops closed, the restaurants closed, and actually if you didn't have a really good reason to be out you were supposed to stay at home. It probably saved us some money, 'cause every time we went somewhere we always found something that we really needed to own.

April 17 –

Billie Strawn died yesterday. Funeral services are going to be for the family only, because of the damn virus. I really hate not going; when we were in high school Billie, Elra Sapp, and me attended a lot of prayer meetings together on Saturday nights. (We'd go somewhere, then pray we could get the hell away from wherever it was without getting hurt.)

April 18 –

Forty-some years ago Marcia said we needed more shelves in the garage. I had fully intended to build them, but I'd been pretty busy. Anyhow, after this crap started I made a materials list, went to the lumberyard, and then spent about a week building a 4-hour set of shelves. My grandson Stephen helped me get a couple of sheets of paneling put up for backing, to keep the insulation from messing up the shelves. Two days after they were finished I had them nearly full of toys that had been piled in closets. Zane came by to check out the project, and after looking it over he remarked, "You've got a shelf and a half still empty, after this virus is gone we need to make some toy runs, no use wasting all of that space."

I mentioned that my daughter-in-law Jamie brought me a mask to wear. Also, my sister Virginia, who lives in Falls Church, VA, sewed up some home-made masks. She sent me one so that I would have one in each truck. Not long after that I received a home-made pink mask from my cousin Roger and his wife Diane who live in Georgia. Their note said, "Your sister and your son were sure you would like to have this." I told Sis, "Dammit, you all are ganging up on me." At least I don't have an excuse not to wear one of the damn things.

Clarence Raup of Hawk Point, MO, is married to Bill Blackwell's niece. He called me last fall and offered to give me his dad's old 960 Ford tractor if I'd come and get it. It would be hard to beat that price so I jumped on it. Greg and I hauled it home and it sat in the barn all winter. We finally got started on it, and I piddle around on it a little bit every day or so. My 670 Moline is still hooked to the brush hog and hasn't been out of the shed since early October. My M5 Moline has a bale spike on it, and I put out hay for Leah's horses a couple of times last winter. I use my little Massey loader tractor occasionally, but I really don't need a tractor very often anymore, however it will still be nice to get another one fixed up and have it sitting around in the way.

I try to get out and walk at least 3 or 4 times a week. Some of the grass-land trails in Rock Bridge Park don't get much use, and the back side of Murial Crane's place, behind all of the City of Columbia soccer fields, is also a good lonesome place to walk. Stephen's Lake, Phillips Lake, and the Devil's Ice Box are all too crowded to suit me. Anyhow, I can usually find a place to walk that's not too civilized.

April 20 –

My Brother-in-law, Bob Wilkerson, and I usually eat supper at Jimmy's Steak House once or twice a month. This virus crap stopped that, now we just talk on the phone occasionally.

I've been mowing the yard more than I normally do, it keeps me busy and it's easy. I just can't get too interested in hard work anymore. The virus hasn't made a real big difference in my life, it's kinda like having hemorrhoids, not really pleasant but I can deal with it. I'm sure if you got laid off from your job, or your kids' school shut down, or you had to work from home it would cause a lot more problems, but most of what I do isn't really affected by it.

April 22 –

Justin and Amanda are working from home and also taking care of Lexi, since her day-care is shut down. Greg is working from home nearly all of the time, and Jamie gets to occasionally, but she has to go in most of the time. She shares the same little office with two other nurses, and she's not real happy about the situation.

April 25 –

I got the hood, fenders, and a new set of headlights for the 960 painted last week. Jamie is going to paint the raised Ford script when she gets time. I've got well over $1,000.00 in that free tractor so far, and we haven't actually done anything to it yet. Oh well!

April 27 –

Besides farm toys I also collect advertising signs, not necessarily farm related, just anything that looks good. I had several of them leaning up in various places, and after this crap started I managed to get most of them hung up in the garage or on the inside wall of my machine shed. At least now I can see them.

May 2 –

Columbia and Boone County are supposed to open back up Monday, May 4th. I stopped at HyVee this morning and I saw more people wearing masks than I've seen in one place up 'til now. Then I drove a few blocks and went in the NAPA store. Not a mask in sight except for mine. I guess auto parts are safer than groceries. I'm surprised that some of Columbia's lower-class citizens haven't been holding up service stations and convenience stores. You can't usually walk right up to the counter wearing a mask and not be questioned. They'll think about it eventually.

Chris Williams set out 9 hives of bees on the farm a couple of weeks ago, some East of the old shed and the rest of them at the edge of the back yard. There's enough stuff blooming right now that they think they've died and gone to heaven. It's fun watching the little buggers, they sure stay busy.

When you listen to the news they talk about the Corona Virus, the Novel Corona Virus, and the COVID 19 Virus. It's no wonder they can't control it, they can't even decide what to call it. My grandson Stephen calls it "Government Bullshit!"

Virus or no virus, we're getting too damn much rain. I'm glad I'm not trying to put in a crop this spring. It's all I can do to keep up with the grass, I mowed the Parsonage yesterday and here at home this morning. It's supposed to rain again, but the sun is shining.

May 3 —

Every toy show that I've been to for the past 3 or 4 years, Larry Pauley has tried to sell me a set of Commemorative Cockshutts that he bought in Iowa nearly 20 years ago. By the time he hits me up I've usually spent all of the money I want to spend at one show, so I've never bought them. There's been no shows since this crap started, so I called him yesterday and he and Vicky brought them by the house this afternoon. We had a nice long visit. Sam Lasley is checking with some dealers he knows, trying to locate a couple of tractors I've been looking for. Shopping over the phone saves a lot of gas, but I'd rather do it the old-fashioned way.

May 5 –

It drizzled-ass rain yesterday afternoon and showered off and on most of last night, 8/10ths of an inch all together. I'm ready for more sunshine. Kathy Vom Saal called yesterday and I talked to her and Fred for probably 30 minutes. It was the first time I've heard from them since this crap started. A big Black Oak fell down back of their house and Fred offered it to me for firewood if I wanted it, but I passed. I've got more here at home that needs cutting than I'll ever get done.

I picked up the gas tank for the 960 from Hager Radiator Service yesterday, they had boiled the rust and crud out of it. Doug Henderson pulled in while I was there, he was driving a 1970's Plymouth Valiant that was freshly restored, it was beautiful. We talked old cars and trucks for quite a spell. He asked if my I.H. pickup was for sale, but it's not.

The new Dollar General Store just West of Millersburg has disinfectant supplies that are impossible to find anywhere in Columbia. I told the clerk that if the store was a little bigger they could put Columbia out of business. I wouldn't care if they did, Columbia's gotten too damn big, I liked it better the way it was back in the 1960's.

May 8 –

I took the 960 sheet metal over to Greg's shop so Jamie can paint the script if it rains. I puttered around out in the shed for a while, then repaired some toy tractors; replaced steering wheels, mufflers, decals, and so forth. I planted some flowers last Sunday, May 3rd. I knew it was a little early but it was so nice out I did it anyway. Now it's supposed to frost tonight. I guess I'll cover the damn things up, they cost too much to replant.

May 10 –

My grandson Sam came by this afternoon and stayed for around 3 hours. He moved from New York City to Castle Rock Colorado just before all of the crap hit. His car and his dog were still in Columbia and he came back to get them. It was the first time I'd seen him for 6 or 8 months and we had a good visit.

Bobby Baumgartner Jr. brought me a printout of the 960 exhaust system and left it with Stephen. Jimmy Riley, the Tennessee barn painter, stopped by and talked to Stephen before I got back from my walk. He comes to Missouri every spring. I guess he figured that barns need painting, virus or no virus. That's more company than I usually have in a week, virus or no virus.

I was mowing the yard Sunday afternoon when the mower started smoking. I headed for a water hose but before I got there smoke boiled out so thick I couldn't see, oil gushed out, and after a few good thump-thumps my recently rebuilt mower became worth whatever it will weigh up for scrap. DAMN! Leah and Ryan came by just in time to hear the last few thumps. Greg called, he heard it from over at his house. He said it sounded like someone blew an engine at a tractor pull.

Stephen is a care-giver. He went to work Saturday night at midnight, and will be there 'til noon on Wednesday. His last shift he was there a full week, so it's getting better. I fried 2 pounds of sausage this afternoon after the mower blew up, and baked a dozen biscuits, that and two or three peanut butter sandwiches should about do me 'til he gets home.

May 11 –

I drove over to Ennis Equipment in Mexico and looked at Cub Cadets this morning. They're not bad, but weren't exactly what I wanted. Zane Dodge told me if I bought a Cub Cadet he'd beat me with a 2x4, I don't think he's too impressed with them. Bill Burnett at Lawn and Leisure in Columbia has a 20 hp Red Max that he thought was just what I was looking for, but it's still in the crate. They're going to put it together and call me.

Walmart's Photo lab is still closed, they don't know when they'll reopen. Some places you see a lot of masks, other places no one is wearing them. I guess if the dumb ones all die off it will upgrade the gene pool.

When Sam was here he said he just had one mask and it wasn't washable. I gave him the one Roger and Dianne sent me. It had 2 strings that tied in the back, and my hands have so much arthritis that I can't hardly tie a knot in front of me where I can see it, much less behind my head, so I couldn't use it anyway. Now it will be put to good use.

May 12 –

Lawn and Leisure had the mower ready by 10:30. I went in and looked at it, bought it, and they delivered it around 1:30. I finished my yard and got the parsonage mowed. It looked like rain the whole time but it held off. John Paul Allen stopped and talked for a while when I was mowing the road bank. He was on his way to Marilyn Brown's to check cattle.

James Ballenger died, graveside services are tomorrow afternoon, May 13th. I really hate damn funerals but I ought to go. Virus or no Virus, things are pretty much as usual. Justin went back to work at the

Nuke Plant last week, everyone there has to wear a mask all day. Amanda is still working from home, they told her she might be doing that until August.

May 14 –

I went to James Ballenger's funeral yesterday. Grave side services only. Some of us wore masks, but the ones who didn't (a bunch) didn't seem too concerned with social distancing. They had a soft voiced woman preacher and the sound system didn't work, no one past the front row heard anything. They needed one of those old-time rear back and holler Baptist Preachers who could tell you that you were going to hell from half a mile away.

The rain is still holding off, it's heavy overcast again, but just a drizzle.

May 15 –

Early morning on the 15th we finally got the rain (1-1/2"), but missed out on the hail and high winds they were calling for. Warm, muggy and overcast, good loafing day. I called Sis yesterday, she's bored but OK otherwise, but my nephew Karl is still pretty sick, it's been over 6 weeks now. He has all the symptoms of the virus but he tests negative. The doctors don't know what the hell is going on.

May 17 –

Heavy overcast, more rain coming. I went over to Greg's this morning. Jamie has the script painted, it looks nice. We pulled one front wheel off so I can get it painted. I'm also going to pack the wheel bearing while it's off. We moved the tractor a little, Jamie and Leah were fussing because it was in front of the hitch rail and they didn't have any place to tie the horses when they washed them.

I prepped and painted the wheel when I got home. It showered a little late evening.

May 19 –

Another cool, cloudy, dreary day. Misted some early. I went to Bob Dudley's this morning and got a haircut, the first one I've had for 3-1/2 months. I got my money's worth. Bob is doing appointments only, one every hour. Zane called and told me Les Hardin died last night. I went and checked the Fortney Cemetery, it's needing mowed pretty bad. I'll try to get hold of Austin Rader this evening.

May 20 –

Another gloomy day. I filled my mower gas cans, stopped by Jeff's for a visit, then went over to Greg's and packed the wheel bearings on the old tractor, and brought the other wheel home for painting. I adjusted the gauge wheels on my new mower, then mowed the yard. Greg Micholson called, his horse pastures need to be brush-hogged. I haven't even changed the oil in my tractor yet, I guess it's about time

May 22 –

Yesterday was another gloomy, misty day. I cleaned up the 960 wheel and painted it, and then mowed at the Parsonage. I stopped at Zane's and visited for a while this morning, then went to Austin Rader's, west of Pierpont. He got a new phone and I couldn't get hold of him. He said he would get the Cemetery mowed before it rained this afternoon. Jamie and Leah came by this evening and brought me a dozen eggs.

May 23 –

I still couldn't get Austin on the phone. I drove down and checked the Cemetery, he got it mowed and it looks really nice. I picked up some health food (ice cream and cookies) at Hy-Vee, nearly everyone was wearing a mask.

May 24 –

Hot and humid this morning. It's turned summer. I serviced the 670 Moline and the brush-hog, then mowed the road bank, barn lot and the patch east of the house. The 670 had been setting in the shed since last October. It started on the first try, not bad for a 54-year-old tractor.

May 26 –

I went over to Greg's and mowed Leah's horse pastures after lunch yesterday, then ate supper with them, Greg had caught a nice mess of Bluegill. It rained ½" late yesterday evening.

I went to Walmart this morning and got some stuff. The S.O.B.'s that are too dumb to wear masks don't know what 6-feet is either. Bunch of idiots! I've been out of reading material so I went to Veranda Antique Mall and found some good mysteries. For the past couple of weeks I've been reading Time-Life educational books.

May 29 –

We had another ½" of rain over the last 2 days. I sat down in my Lazy-Boy yesterday evening and it kinda collapsed. The damn thing wasn't but 29 years old, nothing lasts anymore.

I went to Missouri Furniture this morning and bought a Flex-Steel. Stephen and I moved it into the house, then

I mowed at the Parsonage. It was still a little bit soft, but at least it's done.

May 30 –

My Grandson Clint called me yesterday and said that he and Kat, who live in Festus, MO., were coming to Fulton today to see Kadi, and they wanted me to come over. Justin, Amanda, and Lexi were there, we ate pizza, then watched the space launch. I took Justin the rest of the stuff for my book. I'm going to mow the yard tomorrow if it doesn't rain.

June 1 –

I mowed the yard yesterday, the ground had settled up and wasn't muddy. I painted the gas tank for the 960 after lunch.

I mowed Greg Michalson's horse pastures this morning, it took 3 ½ hours. Greg planted his sunflower patch for the doves this afternoon. Walmart's photo lab is still closed so I got some copies made at Walgreen's at Providence and Broadway. A few hours after I was there a bunch of dumb-assed protesters vandalized the place. There was a swarm of bees in the pine tree in the back yard this afternoon.

June 2 –

I took a walk early while it was still cool, on the back side of Murial Crane's place (now a city park). I saw five people and 1 dog, well spaced out. I went to Tractor Supply and got some new overalls, then un-covered the A.C. compressor and started the A.C. after I got home. It's supposed to get hot this week and I figured it was time.

David Grant is baling hay. McGowen Farms no-tilled beans across from my house yesterday afternoon and this morning. They spread fertilizer, sprayed planted and were gone in 2 days. When I was crop farming it would have taken me a long, hard week to get it done. Of course the planter they had probably cost more than all of the machinery I owned put together. Everything's relative.

June 3 –

My nephew Karl's finally starting to feel a little better. He's had it for over 6 weeks. The Doctors said he's not contagious anymore, and he's getting out of the house and walking a little. He's real weak, the virus or whatever it was really pulled him down.

I went to G&J Auto this morning and got the lights repaired on the back of my old Dodge. Also got it lubed. The temperature got up to 90° this afternoon, the 1st really hot day of the year. There was up to 4" of rain in the Paris-Mexico area last night. We had 1-4/10" by 6 A.M., that beats the hell out of 4".

June 4 –

Those four cops in Minneapolis who choked that black man to death ought to be prosecuted, then hung from the nearest tree. But even that wouldn't pacify the idiots who are protesting all over the country. Some of them are actually protesting the man's death, but a lot of them just see it as a good chance to raise hell and vandalize something. Two people got hit by cars while protesting in Columbia yesterday. If you're going to walk in the middle of the street you ought to expect that. I really don't feel sorry for them. At least a lot of the protesters were wearing masks, they've got more sense than those idiots down at the lake last weekend.

I went over to Zane's for coffee this morning and while I was there I bought a Ford Model 101 3-bottom plow from him; actually from his step-son, Mike Hardin. It had originally belonged to Larry McCray's uncle, Ray

Stephens. It will make a perfect garden/food plot plow on the 960 when we get it finished. During the late 1960's I plowed a lot of ground with a 960 Ford Tractor and a 101 plow.

June 5 –

It showered some last night. I picked up Zane and we went to Mike's house east of Stephens and I paid him for the plow. On the way back we stopped at Artichoke Annie's Antique Mall and walked around. Nothing really interested us, most prices were too damn high.

June 6 –

Stephen went in to work at 7:00 A.M., he won't get off 'til 11:00 Sunday night. More peanut butter sandwiches.

It's supposed to get hot as hell this afternoon. I caught a little green frog in the bathroom this morning and took him back outside where he belongs. I did a bunch of "woman stuff" early; ran the dishwasher, did a load of laundry, changed my sheets, exciting and challenging! Lots of dew early, I mowed the yard after it dried off.

June 8 –

Hot as hell yesterday, about all I did was read. I took an article I'd written for Vintage Tractor Digest over to Greg's yesterday evening and gave it to Leah. She's going to type it for me.

Had two more swarms of bees passed through mid afternoon.

I mowed the parsonage early this morning before it got hot. I went to the Bank, Drug Store and Walmart, then wound up at the Midway Antique Mall. Bought a tractor and a couple of pieces of machinery.

I took the 960 wheels over to Greg's after supper and we got them back on the tractor. There is supposed to be a lot of rain move in tonight and tomorrow, the aftermath of a tropical storm.

June 9 –

It started raining around 2:00 A.M. and had rained 2 ½" by 10:00 A.M. when it finally slowed down to a light mist. Quite a bit of water had started coming in the basement, it's a good thing that it quit when it did. Bob called around 8:00 A.M., he knew the rain was coming so he put in around 12 hours yesterday, mowing yards. He was ready for a little rest.

I went over to Greg's around 4:00 and sat and offered helpful advice while he replaced some of the electrical components on the 960.

June 11 –

I helped Greg on the old tractor for a while yesterday, after supper.

I went over to Murial Crane's place and took a walk early this morning, before it got hot. Marcia's cousin Warren Newton called me, his mom died, she was 96. I also saw in the paper this morning that Joyce Jones' mom died, she was 99. Those 2 ladies must have done something right. Zane brought the plow over around 5:00, Greg unloaded it with his Massey loader tractor. Apparently 101 plows held their value pretty good. I paid $325.00 for a new one in 1967, and $300.00 for this one last week. Zane is going to start mowing hay tomorrow. The beans across the road are up.

June 12 –

I took another walk early, then stopped at HyVee and mailed a box of Kids books to my 3 great grand-kids in Fort Riley Kansas. Chris Williams came by and worked with his bees for a while.

June 13 –

The strawberries are ripe, the cherries are ripe, and the mulberries are ripe, every time I go outside I have a snack. Stephen left for work around 6:30 A.M., He'll get off Sunday night at 11:00 P.M. Clint and Kat drove down to Greg and Jamie's yesterday evening. I spent most of the day at Greg's. Nick Leslie was there, Leah and Ryan, and Justin, Amanda, and Lexi. We found out Kat is pregnant. HOT DAMN!

June 14 –

Beautiful weather. I mowed the yard and brush-hogged the barn-lot early, then visited with Clint and Kat for a few minutes before they left for home. Tractors are running everywhere you look, bean planting should about wind up this week.

June 16 –

Nice again yesterday. I got the M5 out of the shed and washed the dust and bird poop off of it. Another 50-some-year-old tractor started after setting for 6 months.

Clear and low humidity this morning, perfect hay weather. I moved some old bales off of the gravel pad to make room for some new hay for Leah's horses. The dumb-assed protesters are still at it in town.

I got my CDL renewed this afternoon, the License Bureau was a pain in the ass, as usual.

June 17 –

I went to HyVee this morning at 9:00 for coffee with a bunch of retired plumbers and pipefitters from Local 317. It's the 1st time we've gotten together since the shit hit back in March. There were 5 of us, there used to be 8 or

10. It felt kind of weird being out without a mask, even if they did just allow four to a table.

David Grant mowed my hay this morning. After lunch I painted three 50-pound Ford weights that we're going to use on the 960.

Stephen bought a bicycle this afternoon.

June 18 –

Beautiful morning. I went to the Parsonage at 7:00 A.M. and mowed while it was still cool. I painted the rear wheel weights for the 960 when I got back. They're off of a VAC Case but we're going to make them work.

Local governments are removing Confederate statues all over the country. There are a hell of a lot of thin-skinned people in the world, if you look at the dumb son-of-a-bitches cross-eyed they take offence. SCREW 'EM! At least the President of M.U. had the balls not to remove the statue of Thomas Jefferson. He was presented with a petition asking for its removal, but he said it was history and pretty much told them to kiss-off.

David raked the hay this morning and started baling around 4:30 P.M. It needed another 4 hours of sun, but it's supposed to rain tomorrow, and moldy hay beats the hell out of rained-on hay.

June 19 –

Overcast and muggy but no rain yet. I stockpiled 12 of the best bales for Leah's horses and bunched the rest in trailer-load lots, so David doesn't have to chase them all over the field when he starts hauling. Had 24 bales at home and 38 at the parsonage. Good Hay. I took the 670 and the brush-hog to the parsonage and mowed the lagoon bank and trimmed up around the edge of the field in a place or two. It looks better, but I pissed off a bunch of rabbits. David hauled the hay this afternoon. He got done around 4:30 and it started raining a little after 5:00.

June 20 –

Stephen had to work an extra shift this weekend. He went in last night at 11:00 and won't get off 'til Sunday night at 11:00. From 5:00 yesterday evening 'til 7:30 this morning it rained 8/10". More on the way. I baked biscuits and fried enough hamburger and sausage to last the weekend. I hate to cook more than once or twice a week.

I went to Walmart and got a few things I needed and they actually had one whole aisle display full of masks. They weren't cheap, but they're the 1st ones I've found for sale since this crap started in March. About 2 weeks ago I left some film at Walmart to be developed. The guy working in the photo lab said it would be ready today. When I went to pick it up I was told the lab in St. Louis. has been closed because of the Virus and it might be another week. That 1st dummy that I talked to didn't know his ass from a hole in the ground. I should have taken it to Walgreens to begin with.

June 21 –

It rained another 8/10" yesterday afternoon and last night. Mostly clear and real muggy this morning. It was wet, but I mowed the yard. Jeff called and wished me happy Father's Day. Jamie brought me a sack full of homemade molasses cookies. Her and Greg came over late afternoon and visited for a while.

My nephew Karl is slowly getting some strength back. They finally confirmed that he did have the virus. It sure knocked him on his butt.

June 23 –

Not much went on around here yesterday. I went to D&H Drug this morning and got some refills (Drive-through window only), then went up to the Parsonage and cut some sprouts off of the lagoon bank and Tordon'd them. David is mowing hay on Luke's place today. John Paul got the west side of the old Murphy place baled. Lots of hay has been put up the past couple of weeks. I went to Murial Crane's place around noon and walked for a while, then stopped at Moser's and got a bucket of chicken. I'm still not ready to sit down in a restaurant amongst a bunch of people and eat, but I've got no problem with taking it home.

June 24 –

David baled most of Luke's hay today. I talked to Austin Rader, the Cemetery is about ready for another mowing.

June 25 –

Pretty slow around here. David finished Luke's hay and started on Bandy's. I picked up some film at Walmart, they finally got it done. More people are wearing masks than usual, the up-tick in cases must have got their attention. The protesters are finally running out of steam, but they're still yapping about the Thomas Jefferson Statue. DUMB ASSES!

June 26 –

Hot and muggy, I walked early, then stopped at Midway Antique Mall and bought a book about Quantill's Raiders. Stephen is working the weekend over-night shift again.

June 27—

Heavy overcast, muggy, it's fixing to rain. I baked biscuits, fried 2 pounds of sausage and scrambled a dozen eggs after I got up, so I'm good for a few days. It rained 2/10" around 9:00 A.M. I put the decals on the 960 hood after lunch. It rained another 2/10" during the night. Lynn Chandler called this evening, Gary is in the hospital, he has pneumonia.

June 28 –

Cloudy, high humidity, it's gonna get hot today. I've never seen the damn moles as bad as they are this year. My yard looks like a bunch of hogs have been rooting in it. It's a shame the virus doesn't kill moles. I talked to Zane on the phone for probably 30 minutes this morning, he's baled over 400 bales so far this summer. I went over to Greg and Jamie's for supper, Greg had caught a mess of channel cat.

June 29 –

Mostly sunny, windy, no dew. I mowed at the Parsonage then took my gas cans to Millersburg and filled them. It came a hard shower around 4:00, rained 3/10". Stephen fried pork loin and potatoes for supper.

June 30 –

Overcast, hot and muggy this morning. I had a dentist's appointment, I'm good for another 6 months. Wore a mask in, they unlocked and let me in, then locked the door behind me. Different! I was going to mow the yard when I got home, but it showered. David hauled hay from Luke's place today, until it rained.

July 1 –

Heavy overcast early, it started raining around 8:00 A.M. I talked to Lynn yesterday, Gary got out of the hospital Sunday, she said he's really weak. Bev Blackwell called yesterday, she's done with chemo for now, but they're starting her on another round of radiation treatments, and immune therapy. She said she's feeling pretty good, considering.

It rained 3/10" this morning. The sun came out around 1:00, so I went ahead and mowed the yard. The ground was solid, but the big-assed mole hills were real muddy, I had to go around them.

July 2 –

I went over to Greg's yesterday evening after supper and we made a list of parts I need to get for the 960 at NAPA. One of these days we're going to have that thing where we can try to start it.

Zane picked me up around 9:00 and we drove down to Carl Rhodes' Toys S.W. of Linn. I got a couple of tractors I've been looking for and Zane found a 560 Farmall he wanted. We came back through Hermann, then drove through the bottom and North to Fulton. It was the 1st time we'd been out since this crap started, and we had a fun trip.

July 3 –

Partly cloudy, hazy and warm this morning. I went to the Cemetery early, it wasn't mowed. I stopped by Austin's house around 9:00 A.M. and got him out of bed. He said he'd get it mowed today. I finally got his new phone number.

I went by Orscheln and the bank, then went to NAPA and got another $100.00 worth of parts for the 960. I went to HyVee and got some hotdogs and buns for

Jamie's 4th of July shindig. Everywhere I went except NAPA most people were wearing masks and doing the anti-social distancing. Around 4:00 we had a pretty good thunderstorm, and it showered off and on 'til after dark. Rained about 3/10" Between 8:00 and 11:00 it sounded like a war zone around here, the neighbors pissed away a lot of money on firecrackers.

July 4 –

Partly to mostly cloudy early. Stephen is pulling another 48-hour weekend shift. I went over to Greg's around noon, Clint, Kat, Justin, Amanda, and Lexi all came, Leah and Ryan were there, and Ryan's cousin and his girlfriend. We had hamburgers and hotdogs, then Lexi and Amanda rode the new pony. Eventually everyone except me went to the pond swimming. I came home and took a nap. I talked to Taylor for a while this morning, they wanted to come but Fort Riley limited everyone to 70 miles from the base. Kristin called and wished me a happy 4th. She was in Kansas.

July 5 –

Beautiful sunshine this morning, it's supposed to get really hot today. No Missourian again this morning, the guy I talked to when I called in agreed this is almost getting to be a habit. He's going to see what he can do about it. I went over to Greg's for a late breakfast, then Clint and Kat stopped by the house for a few minutes on their way home.

David Grant is hauling bales from Luke's today. I talked to Lynn this evening, Gary is still pretty weak, but he's feeling better.

July 6 –

David stopped and talked for a while this morning. He's going to Mow on Bandy's today. I went to Tractor Supply, then swapped some books at Veranda Antique Mall. I cleaned out under the lawn mower deck and greased the mower after I got home. It's gonna be hot this afternoon. Tom Grant's been cutting wheat on the Lanham Place. Tim Darling from Water District #9 brought me a sample bottle this afternoon. Every so often the district has to take x number of samples at random from their customers, to satisfy the BATF or EPA or some-such nosy Government Agency. Water would be cheaper if there were fewer regulations.

July 7 –

The Missourian was laying on the ground about 2' from the box this morning. This is getting to be bullshit. The firecracker wars got out of hand over the holiday. Five people were shot near Lake of the Woods, a woman and an 11-year-old girl were killed. A 16-year-old kid was arrested for the shootings. He'll probably stay in Juvenile Detention 'til he's 21, then they'll turn his ass loose so he can do it again. Stupid is getting really prominent around Columbia.

I saw in the paper this morning that Elvin Sapp died. I first met Elvin back in the 70's. I was on the New Haven School Board and we bought 10 acres of El Chaparral subdivision ground from Emery Sapp and Sons to build Cedar Ridge School.

I mowed the yard this morning, finished around 11:00. It was just starting to get hot. It got into the mid-90's this afternoon. I went over to Greg's after supper and we ordered some parts for the 960 from Steiner Tractor Parts. That free tractor is starting to get expensive.

July 8 –

Today is my 78th birthday. When I was crop farming it seemed like I always combined wheat on my birthday. No combining today, but I mowed at the Parsonage early. Sis called and left a happy birthday message on my answering machine while I was mowing. Kristin called right after I got home. I went by the bank and ordered some checks, washed the I.H. pickup, then went to State Farm Ins. and checked on a windshield chip. Jamie called me on her way home from work and said she owed me a birthday cake. Rachel called and the boys said hi, then we talked for quite a spell. I went over to Greg's after supper and we piddled with the old tractor some. It was still pretty hot so we didn't do a whole lot.

Chris Campbell wanted everyone to keep a diary so that 100 years from now people could read them and know what the DamPanic was all about. So now you've read my little portion of the Boone Co. Hist. Society Memory Book, and you're probably thinking "He sure was a grumpy old fart!" Well, being around assholes and idiots will make you grumpy, and no one ever said that Boone County didn't have an over-abundance of assholes and idiots, so at least I came by it honest.

I started writing these notes on April 15th. I suppose I could keep on for another week so that it would be an even three months, but today is my 78th birthday and that seems like a good time to shut it down. I've seen some weird shit happen over the past 78 years, but 2020 probably has more than I've ever seen before. Between the virus, Masks, anti-social distancing and a bunch of damn-idiot protestors laying down in the streets and tearing down historical monuments, this is about as weird as I care to see. The virus will eventually be under control, and the dumb-assed protestors will either be in jail where they belong or setting in a nursing home wondering why they pissed away so much time when they could have been doing something important. If they spent half as much time building something as they do tearing stuff up, there could be some really nice neighborhoods around. But I don't suppose that's ever going to happen.

It's possible this crap will disappear in 2 or 3 months, but I don't look for that to happen. It'll probably be 2 or 3 years before they come up with a vaccine that protects people from it. There has always been something. When I was little me and all the other kids had mumps, measles, chicken-pox and the croup, now you rarely hear of those diseases. Also, parents were almost afraid to let their kids out of the house for fear they would contract Polio, and a lot of kids did. Everyone my age knows at least one person who was crippled permanently by Polio, now that's another disease that you rarely hear about. After COVID 19 is under control something else will come along, and people will just have to learn to deal with it or die. It's been that way forever, and it's not going to change.

I hope reading this will give you a little idea what it was like in Boone County in 2020.

Alan Easley

I'm Done Now

Ever since it first came on the air back in the early 1960s, I've been a fan of "Hee Haw." I still watch the reruns on RFD TV on Sunday nights, I consider it educational television. One of my favorite segments is "Hee Haw's All Jug Band." Minnie Pearl plays the piano, and Misty Rowe, Lisa Todd, Ronnie Stoneman, Lulu Roman and maybe a couple more all play homemade instruments of some sort. When they're done, Minnie Pearl turns around on the piano bench and says, "We're through playing, NOW!"

Well, I'm through writing, NOW! I hope you enjoyed it.